DANCING SOMM
Life of the Napa and Sonoma Wine Sherpa

"I have attended a couple of Sandrew's wine education experiences. He puts a fresh approach on them that makes it fun and easy to learn more about wine. I highly recommend any of his style and material."

— Colby Smith, Executive Director Concierge Alliance of Napa Valley & Sonoma (CANVAS)

"Sandrew gave the wine tasting experience of a lifetime! The ambiance and table settings in the cave room were second to none. I learned so much from Sandrew… from wine classification (fruit/spices/other characteristics), to proper techniques on experiencing each wine's unique bouquet and tasting. The wine & food pairing question/answer segment stimulated great audience participation. I've learned the magic of thinking outside the box to creatively pair my wine with dishes I traditionally would not pair with. It was so amazing and mysterious to experience how each wine evolved differently during the event. It was also fun sharing my experiences with the other guests as each had their own opinions to add. I felt very comfortable with Sandrew. Kudos to you for an unforgettable experience. Mahlo."

— Troy Vienagas, Hawaii

"Sandrew is a very knowledgeable wine professional. His ability to educate the customer and engage them in the tasting process was highly skilled."

— Sil Coccia, Director of Hospitality and Consumer Sales Jarvis Estate Winery

"My group comes to Wine country every year and we really wanted to have a whole new experience. Sandrew delivered a most unique experience with his vast array of knowledge and whimsical anecdotes – kind of an insider's scoop – and the wines – really impressive! I'm a CEO and have little time to build my prized wine cellar. Now I have one source I can rely on for all my wine."

— Don Goens, Chicago

"This was such a blast! I really love wine and I'm a foodie. I thought I had a pretty good handle on this whole wine and food thing but Sandrew's Food and Wine Seminar raised the bar several notches up!" – Erik Stenson, Sausalito "Wow! What a great education!! We are still talking about the wines and the Seminar 3 weeks later…"

— Mike Tatom, Denver

"I travel a lot for business and get to eat out often at some of the world's best restaurants with great wine lists so I'm a bit spoiled. This whole evening that Sandrew and his staff put together was truly 0awesome! The pairings were spot on and the flavors – over the top! But now I understand and not just that they go together, but how and why they go together. I'm inspired to get in the kitchen!"

— Greg Barnes, San Francisco

Dancing Somm

Life of the Napa and Sonoma Wine Sherpa

Sandrew Montgomery

Dancing Somm
Life of the Napa and Sonoma Wine Sherpa
All Rights Reserved.
Copyright © 2019 Sandrew Montgomery
v3.0

The opinions expressed in this manuscript are solely the opinions of the author and do not represent the opinions or thoughts of the publisher. The author has represented and warranted full ownership and/or legal right to publish all the materials in this book.

This book may not be reproduced, transmitted, or stored in whole or in part by any means, including graphic, electronic, or mechanical without the express written consent of the publisher except in the case of brief quotations embodied in critical articles and reviews.

Outskirts Press, Inc.
http://www.outskirtspress.com

ISBN: 978-1-9772-0405-9

Cover Photo © 2019 Kat Montgomery. All rights reserved - used with permission.

Outskirts Press and the "OP" logo are trademarks belonging to Outskirts Press, Inc.

PRINTED IN THE UNITED STATES OF AMERICA

Foreword

This book, like most of my life, is rather unconventional.

I have had the great fortune to truly "Live Le Reve".

For years my guests and clients have been asking me to write a book with my signature recipes. As flattered as I was, I didn't want to just write a cook book per se. Plus, it would be rather short. However, I do have a lot of stories about the incredible California wine pioneers who I have had the great fortune of working with and for, including Robert Mondavi, Peter Mondavi, Francis Ford Coppola, Christian Moueix, Eileen Crane, Jack Davies, Charlie and Chuck Wagner, John Shafer, Donald Hess, Merry Edwards, Tony Terlato, Gil Nickel, Robert Sinskey, Ray Signorello, Sandra McKeiver, Frank Altimura, Joe Heitz, Clarke Swanson, Ramona Nicholson, Mike Benziger, Jeff Kunde, Bruce Cohn, Tom Mazzocco, Marimar Torres, Sam Sebastiani, Jess Jackson, Bill and Will Phelps.

Over my 40 + years in the wine industry I have taken to heart the wisdom and knowledge that these dynamic wine visionaries have imparted to me as mentors. Here within these pages will be some of those nuggets and some of my proprietary intellectual property that I have developed since having become a Wine Educator and Sommelier since 1982.

I in turn have been delighted to play to audiences of one to thousands, sharing these insights and observations , as there are NO hard and fast rules when comes to the world of wine. Rather, they are "suggestions" in how to approach and appreciate wine to elevate one's experience.

And in so doing, have come to meet people from all walks of life-Rock Stars, comedians, Movie Stars, celebrity chefs, politicians and major professional sports figures. All because of wine. Wine brings us together to share inspired conversations, learn of new gastronomic delights, creates new friendships and strengthen human bonds like no other libation or anything else for that matter. After all, it is a beverage of pleasure!

So this is a book about wine and food pairings, how tos and whys, recipes, anecdotes, the Golden Years of the California Wine Industry, famous people and a very lucky guy, who has had the great fortune to be the Napa and Sonoma Wine Sherpa, guiding folks for 4 decades through new wine ventures, livin' le reve (living the dream) as the Dancing Sommelier.

I want to thank Nancy and David Padberg for being my advocates and the ones who nudged and encouraged me to finally get all these recipes, stories, anecdotes, and histories out of my head and on to paper! I hope you find this to be a good read and that someday I may meet you and share a glass and hear your story!

Table of Contents

1. Livin' LeReve 1
2. "The Eagle Flies" (The Sam Sebastiani story) 8
3. Judgement of Paris: Bottle Shock 14
4. Mondavis 24
5. The Eagle has Landed 30
6. 9ers Dude! 34
7. Demystifying the "Flavor Profile" 38
8. California Wine Marketing 87
9. Back to San Francisco 98
10. Grateful 101
11. Crazy Horse (The Neil Young story) 109
12. Sonoma Ambassador 111
13. Pinot Passion, The Benzigers,
    Biodynamic Farming Practices and More 132
14. Paintball Wars 137
15. Audacious Scandalous Scoundrel 142
16. Defending Merlot - the "Sideways" effect 152
17. The Napa Valley Jazz Getaway 158
18. "Terroir", "Tannin", "Flavor Profile", "Balance" –Explained 166
19. Jess Jackson, Maverick; Matanzas Lavender 170
20. Carneros and the Chateau on the Plateau 174
21. Visualize Whirrled Peas 178

Recipes

Reggae Rasta Prawn Pasta con Limon EVOOdo Sauce 45

Classic Classical Whole Roasted Chicken Provencal 47

Shakin' Seared Sea Scallop Shuffle 48

Dancin' Duck Breasts confit with Grand Marnier infused cherries
and Asian 5 spice 51

Soulfulfilling Creamy Wild Mushroom Risotto 52

"Jammin' Slammin' Salmon" 53

Prescient Pear and Punk Pomegranate Salad 58

Texas Two-Step Terrific Teriyaki Tri Tip 59

Rhythm and Blues Barbeque Baby back Ribs 60

Boysenberry Hoisin Sauce 61

Yam Frites Shakin' with Asian 5 spice 63

Struttin Leg o' Lamb with Rosemary Dijon Mustard Crust
and Wild Mushrooms 64

Rockin' Moroccan Glazed Carrots with Pine Nuts and Olives 68

Bebop Beat Beets 70

Whole Roasted Sashaying Sea Bass 72

Curried Coconut Lemon Cucumbers 73

Kickin' Killer Krab Kakes 74

Mango Tango Salsa Salsa! 76

Succulent Swingin' Swordfish 78

Tap Dancin' with Tapenades 79

Green Olive Tapenade 80

Sandrew's Sufferin' Summer Succotash 81

Hip-Hop Jicama/Pear Slaw 83

Double Cut Brined Pork Chops 84

Bootylicious Braised Brussel Sprouts 85

Wonderful Waldorf Hysteria Salad 86

1

Livin' LeReve

"The Life of <u>The</u> Napa and Sonoma Wine Sherpa"

I have had the great fortune and honor to have helped launch or be involved with some of California's most noble wineries and have had a helluva lot of fun telling their stories. In the course of 40 years, I have had the great pleasure of working with some of the industry's luminaries and pioneers, and in the course of that, because of that, meeting and serving many famous people in the Entertainment Industry as well.

I grew up in Washington D.C. from John F. Kennedy's assassination to the Watergate scandal, and everything in between. That would include seeing the Beatles at RFK stadium at 6 years old, the assassinations of Martin Luther King, Jack and Bobby Kennedy, the Civil Rights movements, riots, demonstrations, protests of the Vietnam War by the hippies and Yippies, and Woodstock. It was here I met John McCain, as his step son Doug McCain was in my class, along with Timmy Shriver and where I also experienced my first crush on a girl his sister, Maria Shriver.

In 1977, I went to the University of Denver (DU) for Hotel and Restaurant Management School. That is where I experienced my first professional wine tasting-I was fascinated, but never thought it would be the start of shaping what has turned out to be my "le reve" (French for " the dream"). I was hell bent on owning my own restaurant (so I thought). My first gig out of college was managing a French restaurant called the One-Up in downtown San Francisco in 1981, when I didn't know much about wine, and Geoff, the Sommelier there was *very* quick to point that out to me! "Look out the window-an hour away is Wine Country-we should go"….

And so it began. My first true Wine Country experience. Now I had been to Firestone Vineyards tasting room in Santa Ynez with some college buddies, but, as you might imagine, this was more about free alcohol. So Geoff took me on my first serious wine adventure, driving us to Sonoma County's Gundlach Bundschu (affectionately called "GunBun" by insiders) where Jim Bundschu was conducting the tour and tasting that inspirational day. Jim greeted us with a glass of Riesling, which was right up my alley since that is the wine that I drank the most at D U and was very comforting in this overwhelming and intimidating subject matter. He told us that his Grandfather had advised him and his brother to "never plant Riesling over here- it's too hot! And don't try to grow Cabernet over there- it's too cold". The brothers promptly dismissed their wizened Grandfather thinking 'Ah what the hell does the old man know!' Laughing, Jim admitted that after trial and error and several years of failure by doing just the opposite, that Grandpa was right all along. Jim cracked a lot of jokes that day while pouring really delicious wines-in fact, he was funny as hell! And, I'm pretty sure he was *not* spitting. He took us in to the winery for a final barrel sample. I noticed on the wall a poster, with a 1950's police squad car and a Barney Fife look-alike in a Mayberry's sheriffs' uniform with the caption: "If you can't pronounce Gundlach Bundschu Gewurtztraminer, you haven't had enough to drink!"

I drove home that day inspired by Jim Bundschu thinking to myself, "who the hell needs to open "Sandrew's" restaurant if you can have this much fun in the wine business?"

Now I needed a strategy, but I didn't know how to go about it. I have to admit I wasn't entirely happy with my work situation. At age 22, I was naive enough to think that I could just cut off my long hair from college, don a 3-piece suit and *somehow* I would be transformed and ready for the corporate world. HA!

I have to admit it was pretty cool that on my first day at the One –Up, that my third guest was the then Mayor of San Francisco, now long-time Senator Diane Finestein. Not to mention the access to Wine Country. It was so close-just an hour away and there was something up there that entranced me, almost a beckoning. "More education", I thought to myself: "this will be my graduate school."

My next trip took me to Napa. I was going to Beringer. My sister Midge had turned me on to their Chenin Blanc-that was big back then. I drove through the compact City by the Bay over the Golden Gate Bridge and continued on Highway 101 into Marin County, until I noticed what had been a suburban sprawl all of a sudden became wide open spaces. There were cows grazing all around and the Bay was still visible to the right, but I was definitely out of the City. Fascinated with how abruptly this occurred. I almost missed the turn off to Highway 37, but then I noticed a sign: "Napa/Sonoma"-Shit! I better get over fast! And I was on my way-to NAPA! The Napa Valley. It sounded *magical,* and man, was I excited. Taking the turn up to Highway 29, I was taking it all in. On my way there was a big wooden sign: "Welcome to this world famous wine growing region Napa Valley".

I continued up Highway 29, passing vineyards on the left and right. Where one vineyard ended, the next one began, almost seamlessly. I drove through the pretty little town of St. Helena and then popped out on the other side of town where the nonstop vineyards began again. I continued on the road until I saw the old metallic sign for Beringer Brothers Winery on the right, pointing to the left.

I turned in and right there was that beautiful brown German castle.

So this is how it is, I thought to myself, how spectacular!

While I was enjoying my tasting, the lady pouring the wines seemed interested in talking to me, describing the wines and doing a good job of asking questions to gauge my level of wine knowledge. She told me about this event that had taken place only a few years earlier in France, and there was a book about it called <u>The Judgement of Paris</u>. Pretty cool, I thought to myself and here I thought the California wine industry had been around for over a hundred years! Well it had been, but there was prohibition and before that phylloxera destroying many of the vineyards. Much of the Napa Valley had been replanted to plum tree orchards for that wonderful elixir called prune juice and there were many walnut groves and cattle ranches as well. *If* Americans were drinking wine, it most likely was out of carafe. Restaurants would offer you the House Chablis (mostly mediocre Chenin Blanc and French Columbard-no Chardonnay at all), Burgundy (most likely Ruby Cabernet-no Pinot Noir to be found here) or Rose' (often a blend of the former two).

Until that Judgement of Paris thing…

"When did you say that tasting took place?" I asked her.

"1976. You should read the book-it's what put Napa on the map!" she replied enthusiastically.

1976, I thought to myself, well that was *just* one year before my first seriously organized wine tasting by my instructor at DU. Far out!

I had a very nice wine tasting that day at Beringer, even if I was a bit disappointed they were not pouring their Chenin Blanc that day, if you can believe that! (LOL)

Not sure if I went to another winery that day-there were not many tasting rooms back then. I do recall on the drive back to San Mateo that there was something so right about this for me; it was very appealing. But how do *I* become a part of this?

I lived and commuted from Burlingame and there was a great wine shop on Broadway Street called Weimax. The proprietor there was Gerard and he could see I was sincere about my endeavor and quest for knowledge. He was a very serious fellow and I'm not sure he knew how to take my enthusiasm for my new found hobby. I would try and visit him once a week to extend my thirst and acquisition for knowledge. On Saturdays, he would open a few wines from around the world-countries I had heard of, but mostly from a map. His selection was quite extensive in French classics of course, but he prided himself in discovering these new up and comers from California.

It seemed whatever money I had left over from my apartment rent, gas and car payments, I spent on Gerard's tastings and would buy an occasional bottle.

As I became more disillusioned with the corporate world and the tough urban City life, I was feeling a bit lost. Wondering if I had made the right decision to leave Colorado, I started communicating with an old girlfriend. Maybe I should move back? And so I did.

As a young man, I had developed an expertise in opening restaurants. I had already been a sommelier for Duggan's in Denver and Bennigan's in Aurora, Colorado, but I was interested in getting back into management. I was tapped to open Joe Kelly's Oyster Docks, first in Oklahoma City, then Aurora and finally in Lakewood, just to the west of Denver. In two years' time, I opened these three and was starting to get burned out on this 16 plus hour a day business. I was the Wine Director, Sommelier and Assistant Manager for the Lakewood store which afforded me to go to many trade wine tastings and meet lots of folks in the wine business. My rep from Western Davis Distributing let me know there was an open position in the restaurant division and that I should interview with his boss.

'Ah whatthehell. Can't hurt to interview, right?' But I was still planning on starting my own restaurant and I was still learning on someone else's dime, but I wasn't quite as hell bent as I had been.

So on a Friday in 1985, I took the interview with Mr. Sancerre, the supposed name of the manager who this position would report to. The first question was, "Do you know what my name stands for?"

"Sauvignon Blanc from the Loire Valley", I responded.

"Good. Very few know that." Was the curt reply back setting the tone. (I think I may have passed the test already at this point, but the interview continued on.) By the end, I was made an offer. "Thank you very much! I'd like to discuss this with my wife and get back to you-Monday ok?" "Sure, but no later than Monday. I have others in the wings."

With that, we shook hands and I walked out feeling very confident and good about the interview. But is this what I *really* wanted to do? I mean, I wanted to get into the wine business, but I would be selling spirits as well. Hmmmm...

Per usual, I went to work that night at 4:00 pm. We had an incredible Happy Hour:

2 fer 1 cocktails, free all you could eat 'peel n' eat' shrimp, and 25 cent oysters. I was not only a manager, I was a real Motha Shucka!

One of my bartenders called me over and in a low voice said, "I already cut that guy off on the bar stool, but he wants to talk to a manager." So I sucked it up, let out a fairly big sigh and approached the inebriated man. He proceeded to tell me he wanted another drink and didn't appreciate nor understand why my "Asshole Bartender" wouldn't give him one. I talked to him for a minute or two in a *very* calm voice so as not to escalate the situation. As he started to slide off the stool, it was obvious he wanted to throw a punch. What he didn't realize was, what was happening behind him. When you are still in the opening few weeks of a restaurant, you have double the staff. Twelve cooks filed out of the kitchen into the bar and lined up right behind him in their pristine clean Chef Whites with arms folded, all of whom had the look of "Go ahead, buddy. Throw the first punch!"

That was it. That was the turning point. That was all I needed to see. That was a microcosm of my future if I were to stay in the bar business.

"Think I'm gonna take that offer after all." I said to myself. "I don't need this shit!"

And so I finished out the weekend with the relaxed mindset and knowledge that I would call Mr. Sancerre Monday morning, accept and give my 2 weeks notice to Joe Kelly's.

And so began my adventures on the wholesale side of the wine business.

2

"The Eagle Flies"
(The Sam Sebastiani story)

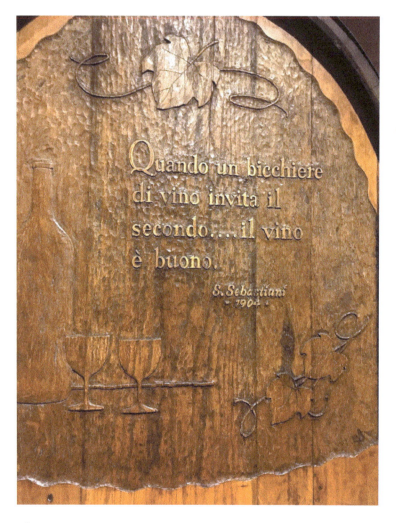

    When I first met Sam Sebastiani at his eponymous winery in Sonoma, he was the President of Sebastiani Vineyards and Winery. He was quite affable and striking in his farmer/ranch hand/cowboy presence. Sam is a third generation

"The Eagle Flies" (The Sam Sebastiani story)

vintner following in his grandfather Samule's (who emigrated from Tuscany in 1895) and father August's footsteps. His mother, Sylvia was the Chairman of the Board. As you might imagine being of Italian decent and a close working family, there was many a "spirited", shall we say, discussion. These folks were of humble origins and yet became Sonoma's biggest winery in terms of volume (tonnage). August and Samuele understood their current respective markets and accommodated the average wine consumer of the day.

During Sam's tenure, he observed how the California Wine Industry was rapidly changing. We as an Industry were growing up, and there was an influx of foreign money coming into Napa. Interest was spilling over into Sonoma County.

Sam grew up in the town of Sonoma very proud of his heritage and family vineyards-especially the prized "Eagle Vineyard", walking distance from his childhood home.

The Eagle Vineyard, now Cherry Block on the Eastern side of Sonoma Town

He felt that the Eagle Vineyard could make their very best Cabernet Sauvignon out of all of their land holdings. With the rise of California's first "cult" wines like Heitz Cellars "Martha's Vineyard", Caymus "Special Selection", Phelps "Insignia" and "Backus", Duckhorn "Three Palms", "Opus One", Dominus Estate", and "Rubicon", Sam thought it was time for Sebastiani to step up and out of the status quo fray. It was time for the Eagle to fly.

Sam made the Eagle Cabernet wine with stunning labels-a magnificent depiction of a Bald Eagle, different each vintage. The wine was powerful, with silky tannins and great concentration of fruit.

I was excited to be on the ground floor of this remarkable endeavor. I didn't care how much I had to spend each year, even though I couldn't afford it-after all, I was in the wine business for god's sakes!

I was going to collect the entire vertical and I did… All 3 years.

"The Eagle Flies" (The Sam Sebastiani story)

As President of the Winery, Sam felt it only appropriate that he arrive and leave in limousines to his appointments, eating luxurious meals, etc. This was part of the new image. After all, Sam's vision was different from his parents and grandparents and *he* was in charge. Sylvia Sebastiani was quickly growing tired of Sam's ambition and desire to change direction from what had made the family business so successful.

In February of 1986, Sam came to Denver to meet with Western Davis' (the Distributor that I was working for) Restaurant Division (on premise) for a dinner at the brand new and exciting Dudley's restaurant. We had a private room and we had been informed that this would be a *very important* meeting with one of our largest and most important suppliers. We all arrived early and Sam was late. Starting to get a little ancy, we started joking about who would be the first to break down and start ordering drinks at the bar. And then Sam Sebastiani opened the door. The atmosphere turned from jovial to tense and nervous. He said nothing- his steely blue eyes at first averted all of ours. He looked down to the floor, then raised his head and put his hands together, cusping them outwardly to us like he was offering his soul to us. Still silence. *This was really getting awkward.* It seemed like almost 10 minutes of this awkward silence. And then, he stated solemnly "My future is your hands."

He asked all of us to open our hands and then cusp them like he did. He proceeded to go around the room and placed a gold medallion with a Bald Eagle on its face in to each one of our hands. When he completed the circle of the room, he reiterated: "My future is in your hands".

And with that, the salad course began being dropped and the Sebastiani wine was being poured and so the evening meeting began. We got the message.

Three weeks later was the next Sebastiani Winery Board meeting. Sam's siblings Don and Mary Ann were present. As Sam presided over the meeting, he called his mother, the Chairman by her first name again. "Sylvia" he began, not realizing how much this irritated her. She interrupted him and said "I am not Sylvia to you, I am your Mother! And as Chairman of the Board I am appointing your brother as President, effective immediately!"

WOW! Just like that, Sam was fired. What was Sam and his wife Vickie to do? Sam believed in his conviction, that he as winemaker and face of the winery should elevate the image and quality of his wine. Thus began "Viansa". Fusing Vickie and Sam's names together. Had a nice ring to it. But he couldn't leverage off the Sebastiani name or marketing arm, so he turned to the Brokerage of California Wine Marketing. I would become the San Diego Regional Manager the very next year.

Viansa's first wines were obvious: Chardonnay, Sauvignon Blanc, Merlot and Cabernet Sauvignon, which initially made sense. That is what Americans were drinking. I had already dubbed America as a "Neopolitan Society" of wine drinkers. Americans for the most part were drinking Chardonnay for the vanilla, Cabernet for the chocolate and White Zinfandel for the strawberry. We were not very adventurous yet...

Reflecting on his proud Italian heritage, Sam once again moved away from the status quo and decided to make wines more true to his roots, producing Pinot Grigio, Primitivo, Sangiovese, and blends thereof and even a Cabernet Franc in homage to his namesake, Samuele. Vicki Sebastiani was quite a talented Chef and started The Market within the pointy tented Viansa selling imported gourmet and domestic food products, including her own signature recipes. The concept of Viansa as not only a tasting room and winery, expanded the brand to tie in wine and food with a pizza oven (innovative at the time) and picnic areas was quite successful. A great getaway for San Francisco Bay Area residents and visitors alike for a quick day trip with its southern Wine Country proximity. However, gradually the toll of husband and wife working so closely together began to erode their relationship and marriage. Viansa was eventually sold. It had a good run. Llyod, the new owner asked me to come in and conduct my Wine and Food pairing seminar for his newly inherited Wine Club members as an event to introduce him, and to make a smooth transition for the future of Viansa.

I had not heard anything about Sam for quite some time other than he had moved and was living in Wyoming or Montana or Kansas. I figured he had had his fill of the wine biz and moved on to "greener pastures". Couldn't blame him.

One day in 2011, while I was working at Kunde Family Estates in Kenwood, where I created their Wine and Food pairing program, there was this gentleman walking about the tasting room. I did a double take at this man who bore a striking resemblance to Sam-those steely blue eyes, but salt and pepper hair. "Sam?" I softly shouted. And sure enough, it was him.

"Are you here for a tasting, Sir?" I asked, half-heartedly, half politely. "What are you up to these days?"

"I'm here because I purchasing some grapes from Kunde for my new wine called La Chertosa, named after the Cathedral in Rome where I was baptized."

"The Eagle Flies" (The Sam Sebastiani story)

Sam stated. "Cool!" I said. "This business is too much in your blood, huh?!" "Yup.", he responded. Then we started talking about the old days…..

"So you'll be here from time to time?" I asked. "Yes" he replied, "still negotiating, but I have been doing business with these folks since the early days of buying Barbera back in the Seventies". I'll be back in a couple of weeks." "Great!" I exclaimed. "I have something for you!"

That night I went home to my dresser drawer and foraged around between the socks and underwear, College diploma and other stuff and there it was. The gold medallion Eagle coin. I had moved from Denver to San Diego to San Francisco to Marin County to Sonoma twice and still had it!

That night I put it in the glove box of my car. A couple of weeks later, Sam showed up to Kunde.

"Sam, will you be here for about 10 minutes?"

"Yeah. Why?"

"'Member I said I had some thing for you? I've got it in my car. I'll be right back."

I went out to my car and brought back the Eagle medallion in its original box into the tasting room.

"Do you remember back in 1986 you came to Denver and we had dinner with our On Premise division?"

"Sort of."

I didn't say anything. I just pulled the box from my pocket and handed it to him.

"Go ahead. Open it." He barely got it open and you could feel the emotion well up and overcome him.

His eyes welled up and a tear came down his cheek.

It had been 25 years!

"Thank you. Thank you for this."

"Good luck with the new endeavor!" I said encouragingly.

3

Judgement of Paris: Bottle Shock

I found out about the "Paris Tasting of 1976" also referred to as the "Judgement of Paris", in 1981. My first professional tasting was in 1977, a mere year after this hugely important historical event. If there was one single event that put Napa and Sonoma on the map so to speak, this was it. This event forever changed the Wine World. Covered by veteran newsman, George M. Taber, who chronicled the tasting and wrote a book about it. Much later (2008) a movie, a loosely based documentary called Bottle Shock was filmed, staring Alan Rickman as the event's producer Steven Spurrier and Chris Pine who began his Hollywood career playing Bo Barrett of Chateau Montelena. It was my first movie to have a little cameo in too.

That day on set, Kat and I had lunch with Alan Rickman and Chris Pine. Alan was a very nice man (and really talked like that!) and down to earth. I spent a good part of the lunch explaining to him the import of this unique and extraordinary event that the Judgement of Paris tasting was and how it shaped my life and career. He graciously acknowledged how important it must have been to me, but my sense was it was just another acting gig for him. I just *had* to be in it,

Judgement of Paris: Bottle Shock

as I have been talking about it as a Wine Educator and sommelier since 1982 and it has always been a focal point of most of my seminars, classes and educational sessions for my Private Chef, Personal Sommelier business.

Spurrier's intention for The Paris Tasting of 1976 on May 24th was to sell more French wine in his Caves de la Madeleine, a wine store he opened in 1970 to show off the best of France and that these wines were in a class of their own and would remain untouched.

However, here are the results:
Average Original grades: out of 20 points.

Rank	Grade	Wine	Vintage	Origin
1.	14.14	Stag's Leap Wine Cellars	1973	USA
2.	14.09	Château Mouton-Rothschild	1970	France
3.	13.64	Château Montrose	1970	France
4.	13.23	Château Haut-Brion	1970	France
5.	12.14	Ridge Vineyards Monte Bello	1971	USA
6.	11.18	Château Leoville Las Cases	1971	France
7.	10.36	Heitz Wine Cellars Martha's Vineyard	1970	USA
8.	10.14	Clos Du Val Winery	1972	USA
9.	9.95	Mayacamas Vineyards	1971	USA
10.	9.45	Freemark Abbey Winery	1969	USA

White wines
California Chardonnays vs. Burgundy Chardonnays **Average** Original grades: out of 20 points.

Rank	Grade	Wine	Vintage	Origin
1.		Chateau Montelena	1973	USA
2.		Meursault Charmes Roulot	1973	France
3.		Chalone Vineyard	1974	USA
4.		Spring Mountain Vineyard	1973	USA
5.		Beaune Clos des Mouches Joseph Drouhin	1973	France
6.		Freemark Abbey Winery	1972	USA

7.		Batard-Montrachet Ramonet-Prudhon	1973		France
8.		Puligny-Montrachet Les Pucelles Domaine Leflaive	1972		France
9.		Veedercrest Vineyards	1972		USA
10.		David Bruce Winery	1973		USA

"Sacre Bleu! Mon Dieux!"

And *that* changed history. Up until then, the French had told the entire world that only the French could make world class wines. And guess what? We all believed them! Until then. This opened up the eyes of the world, that if California could make wines that would rival and even beat the Premier Cru wines of Burgundy and the First and Second growths of Bordeaux, what was the potential for South Africa, Chile, Argentina, New Zealand, Australia and the rest of the world? Even Italy and Spain stepped up their games.

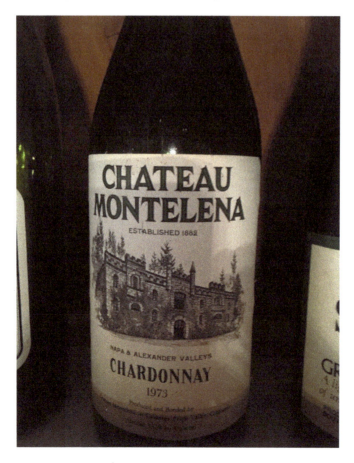

Chateau Montelena's Chardonnay won the contest, its sales took off and was doing exceedingly well. That was all good and fine, but owner Jim Barrett also wanted to be known for Cabernet Sauvignon, after all, this was *the* Napa Valley! It now was very established on the world stage for producing world class Cabernet. I had the good fortune of being part of the wholesale team that re-launched the Cabernet program for Chateau Montelena, so I got to work with Jim, but never got to meet his son, Bo Barrett. However, I did get to meet his wife Heidi Barrett, the only winemaker in the world to make *five* 100 point wines! Heidi and I met at Fantesca Winery on Spring Mountain where she was the wine maker and I was hired by owners Duane and Susie Hoff on a consulting project. During that time, Heidi and I had several discussions, including helping her marketing efforts for her own brand, La Sirena, that the Chateau Montelena Chardonnay *did* turn color "but pink, not brown" (as Dennis Farina's character so eloquently stated "Ah interesting; the color of shit!"), as well as my approach to breaking down the flavor profile and how to teach people to create magical wine and food pairings. "Oh I see. I do every thing before and up until the cork goes *in* the bottle. You do everything once the cork comes *out* of the bottle" Heidi said to me with the satisfaction, that between the 2 of us, we had all the bases covered. She also informed me of brand new wine venture with Bo: Barrett and Barrett.

"I'd *love* to get in on that. When will you be releasing your first wine?" I asked.

"Oh not for a couple of years yet. It's still in barrel. I'll put you on the list." Heidi replied.

"Great! I look forward to it."

Every February, The Napa Valley Vintners and Growers Association puts on a weeklong event, called "Premier Napa" dedicated to the International trade and media. The Valley is a buzz with all kinds of private tastings, dinners in caves, special bottlings and barrel samples-you name it. The week builds up to a crescendo, ending with the Barrel Auction.

IIn 2013, I was invited to the Wine Writers Guild tasting at The Culinary Institute of America (CIA). As I was blind tasting on that Thursday, I looked around the room for fellow colleagues and in the corner, I spotted a very demure man in a handsome sport jacket with a kerchief in it. "*Man* that looks like Steven

Spurrier", I said to myself. I looked just under his lapel, and sure enough, his ' Hello my name is' tag was written 'Steven Spurrier'. Eventually I went over to him and introduced myself and we exchanged business cards.

That night I went home and opened the door and exclaimed "Hey Kat! Guess who I met today?! Steven Spurrier!" Her response? "Well did you take a picture with him?"

"No." I responded somewhat sheepishly.

"WHAT!?" I've known you for over 20 years-this has been your life for 30 whatever the hell it's been-years and you didn't….."

"Honey, Honey, relaaaax. Saturday is the day of the auction, I'll try and take a picture with him."

So Saturday rolls around and I'm back at the CIA for the auction and pouring from barrel our auction lot. Before the barrel tasting, I started working the room, talking to all the people I know and introducing myself to the ones I didn't. I was walking and talking with Phillipe Melka and he was not taking the hint about possibly partnering with him for me to be the sales, marketing and operations guy to counter his winemaking consulting skills. I had to attempt, learning from my blunder with Michael Browne of Kosta Browne. (More on that in the chapter **Sonoma Ambassador**) As I turned the corner, I recall a swashbuckling Jean Charles Boisset almost severing my arm off as I walked by. He was at his flamboyant best, sabering a bottle of his JCB sparkling wine for guests. Quickly passing by them, I came across Bo Barrett at his Chateau Montelena barrel.

"Hi Bo! I'm Sandrew Montgomery. Nice to meet you."

"Oh I know who you are."

"Well how's that Barrett and Barrett wine coming? Heidi told me all about it."

"I've got some right down here by my barrel." Sizing up that I had no glass in hand, Bo said "why don't you go back to your barrel and get your glass?"

So I go running back to my barrel and come bounding back to Bo with glass in hand like a giddy little boy getting to try his first chocolate shake, and lo and behold, there was Steven Spurrier, 3 barrels away!

"Hey Bo-would you mind taking a picture of Steven and me?"

"No-not at all. In fact…" he starts scrolling down on his cell phone, "this is me and Steven about 3 minutes ago".

Of course while he's scrolling down, I'm thinking to myself: 'Hey fool! Get somebody else to take the picture of *all 3* of you!'

Judgement of Paris: Bottle Shock

If only that day on the set of Bottle Shock, I had taken a picture with Alan Rickman and Chris Pine when I had lunch with them! Oh well; got the real deal hanging over my desk in my office.

I felt compelled to stay in touch with Steven, so I sat down and wrote him an e-mail and he responded back:

Dear Sandrew,

Many thanks for your mail. Yes the 1976 tasting does keep its name in the news. It may be even more so, as there is very likely to be a movie written and made by Robert Kamen, who has a superb vineyard and winery in Sonoma County, on the true story, not at all "Bottle Shock." Watch this space.

I am so pleased that you are at Rutherford Hill, a really fine historic property and one that needs to be talked about once more.

Best regards from Mendoza, where I am judging the Wines of Argentina Awards.

Steven.

-----Original Message-----
From: Sandrew [mailto:Sandrew@ie1.com]
Sent: 17 February 2014 18:14
To: Steven Spurrier
Subject: Premier Napa meeting

Dear Steven,

I have been meaning to e-mail you for all most a year now since we met twice at the CIA at last year's Premier events.

You were kind enough to take a picture with Bo Barrett and myself, and I thank you for that.

What I really want to thank you for is having put on the 1976 Paris tasting.
I have been a wine educator and sommelier since 1982 and have had an excellent career in the wine industry, initially inspired by your event. I am sure

```
there are countless individuals in our industry who
also have you to thank!

Not sure that you have received all the credit you
deserve, so on behalf of all us in the California
Wine Industry, a heart felt "THANK YOU" !

I now mange Rutherford Hill and have been chartered
with re-imaging it and taking it to realize its full
potential.

If you have a chance, I would love to take you around
this beautiful property and tell you what are new
plans are.

My best to you,

Sandrew
```

I never mentioned to Steven my little 'don't blink you'll miss it' cameo in <u>Bottle Shock.</u>

When the movie came out, like we had done with <u>Sideways</u>, we asked when Kat and I would go wine tasting at various wineries in Central Coast California and here in Sonoma and Napa, if these movies had an impact or were being talked about in their tasting rooms. Kat was very much a champion of Chardonnay at the time of <u>Bottle Shock</u> hitting the theaters. I hadn't been to Chateau Montelena in a very long time, and she had never been, so it was time. After all, this *was* the Winery that was the main focus of the movie. So I drove us over the Mayacamas Mountains from the Sonoma side, cruising over the swervey Calistoga road from our house on an overcast Tuesday afternoon. As we started toward the very impressive Castle façade, the "WOW!" factor started to hit us in the face.

"Really is impressive, huh?" I said to Kat.

"Yea-uh! Seeing it in the movie is one thing, but being here…"

So in we walked into the tasting room and was greeted by a very pretty blonde who proceeded to pour us a taste of their delicious Riesling. We briefly chatted about being in the industry and exchanged pleasantries. Then I asked, "So is anybody talking about Bottle Shock since…"

I was quickly interrupted by our hostess:

"Let me tell you what's right about Bottle Shock-**5 things**!

Yes Jim Barrett was our owner at the time.

Yes Jim Barrett was our winemaker.

Yes Bo Barrett is his son.

Yes we won for the Paris tasting with our '73 Chardonnay...."

I was so flabbergasted by her response, for the life of me, to this day, I still can't remember what number 5 was.

She seemed to have felt relieved to get that off her chest and then poured the current release Chardonnay. 'All righty then!' We thanked her and then moved down the bar to another host who I had known for a few years.

"Let *me* tell you what's right about Bottle Shock-3 things!" He was quick to say.

("Oh no, not you too", I thought to myself.)

We politely finished our tasting, bought a bottle of the Chardonnay and walked out to the beautiful Japanese gardens to Jade Lake to drink our wine.

It was a very peaceful setting and the afternoon seemed ethereal and disappeared.

"Uh oh. It's quarter to four and they'll close the gates on us at four so we better get a move on", I turned to say to Kat.

As we started up the driveway leading back to the parking lot, I noticed a gentleman in blue jeans walking ahead of us.

"Mr. Barrett?" I called out.

"Yes? Who's that?"

I introduced him to Kat and re-introduced myself, as I had not seen him for over 25 years.

We naturally started talking about the good old early days of the wine business.

In my head, I'm thinking, 'Do I tell him what I just told you? Or not? Do I tell him, or not?' Kept going back and forth through my head. Then I thought, as a business owner myself, *I'd* want to know. So I told him.

"**WHAT?! Don't they understand free PR?**" Jim exclaimed.

I wanted to give him a big ol' bear hug-but he's not of that generation, so I let it go.

If you've seen the movie, you know, clearly *he* did not understand free PR.

A few weeks after this, there was a new tour at Chateau Montelena.

The Bottle Shock tour, where you could get your picture taken with Mr. Jim

Judgement of Paris: Bottle Shock

Barrett himself and a life size cardboard cutout of Bill Pullman, the actor who portrayed him, or a picture with the real Bo Barrett and life size cardboard cutout of Chris Pine, a copy of the movie and a half bottle of the current Chardonnay… hmmm…..not quite sure how that got started.

4

Mondavis

One of my many mentors was Robert Mondavi. I had the good-no make that great fortune to help him on the wholesale side to launch Opus One with Baron Phillipe Mouton Rothschild. We originally launched with the 1979 version, though the first vintage produced was 1978. It was deemed better to start with the '79 as the inaugural release.

Robert of course was highly instrumental in marketing California wine-ALL California wines. He was a great believer in the potential of the Golden State starting in the early days convincing his father, Cesare, to buy the longest running winery in California, Charles Krug in the Napa Valley. His brother Peter was the winemaker and running the production team and facility, whilst Bob was in charge of sales and marketing with his effervescently charming and charismatic personality.

One day he said to me, "Sandrew. You say 'food and wine pairings' like they are two separate entities. Wine *is* food! I think you need to embrace this concept, as wine is a gracious part of life. As we enjoy each other's company at the table, it should be thought of as such."

"Yes Sir." Was my response with all due respect as I was raised as a Southerner. (I probably still had my accent then and said it with a Southern drawl.)

I will always consider him my mentor for that.

While at wholesale distributors Western at Davis in Colorado and JALCo in San Francisco, I worked with Peter Mondavi Sr. and therefore his sons Mark and Peter Jr. Though I never worked with their cousins, Bob's sons Michael Mondavi who I met in Aspen at the Aspen Wine Fest and his brother Tim Mondavi at Premier Napa at the CIA in St. Helena tasting his delicious Continuum from Pritchard Hill out of a decanter.

When Peter Sr. was turning 100 years old, there was an article in the Napa

Register about this monumental event. It was reported that Peter was still coming into the office on a daily basis. Shortly after that, there was a celebration at Krug that I attended. As soon as I spotted him upstairs in the Carriage House, I immediately approached him. I put my left arm around him and leaned into his ear.

"I understand that you are still coming in to the office every day." I chuckled.

He twinkled and retorted in his gravelly, soft accent, "I'm afraid da boys might screw it up!"

"But, Peter. They're in their sixties now. I think they have a handle on it." I fired back.

"Happy Birthday to you!" I smiled and winked at him.

Opus, however was not the first of the Proprietary wines. That credit goes to the genius of Joseph Phelps. In 1974 Mr. Phelps told his wine maker, Walter Schug (who I also had the good fortune of being part of the Distributorship that launched his eponymous winery), that he had a concept where he wanted to make a very special wine every year and to commemorate the vintage's particular distinctiveness by devising a unique name to be only associated with Joseph Phelps Vineyards. Joe thought long and hard about this naming task, even asking his Board of Directors from his construction company that he and his Dad, Hensel Phelps had started in Greely, Colorado. (Interestingly enough, my old sales territory!) He didn't care for any of the names they came up with, so the arduous naming task continued. As the story goes, in his youth Joe was a sailor in the U.S. Navy and that's when he fell in love with wine, travelling the world. His favorites being from France, especially Bordeaux, Burgundy and the Rhone Valley, but he liked the German Rieslings as well. These were to be the initial influences and ultimately the foundation of what was to become a stalwart winery in the Napa Valley's second "Golden Age".

Joe was legendary for many things, including throwing fabulous dinner parties.* Often at these soirees and other functions, Mr. Phelps would don his Naval uniform. On one of these occasions, while he was shaving, he saw the reflection in the mirror reflecting back his medals, emblems and insignias. There it was! "Insignia"! For honor, integrity and distinctiveness. I asked Joe's son, Bill Phelps, who has been the President of JPV for twenty years and now Chairman, how "Insignia" came about.

"Dad's idea was to make the best wine possible for that year. Dad said it could be white, could be Viognier; could be Syrah. Just wanted Walter to make the very best wine, *whatever* Mother Nature gave us for that particular vintage."

As it turned out, the first vintage of Insignia was 1974, which was a great year for Cabernet Sauvignon. So the inaugural blend was 94% Cab Sauv, 6% Merlot. The next year he instructed Walter in the same fashion. The Merlot provided the highest quality grapes in 1975, thus 86% Merlot and the balance C.S. The following year was again a great year for Cabernet Sauvignon, so back to 94%. Looking back after 45 plus vintages of this iconic wine, it seems ludicrous that it would be anything but a Bordeaux blend, even though in most years it would qualify legally as Cabernet Sauvignon. However all it ever has been printed on the label is "Red Wine", allowing for the flexibility to not to have to adhere to California laws governing a minimum of 75% of the respective varietal in order to qualify to state it on the label. (BTW, this changed in 1983 when the minimum was a mere 51%-which absolutely makes no sense to me.)

That 1974 Insignia was made up at Joe Heitz' place, as the Phelps winery was still under construction and had no wine making equipment yet. Joe and Joe, as opposite personalities as they were, were very good friends. In fact it was Joe Heitz who christened the Phelps property with an 1864 Madeira.

Bill tells the story about that first vintage.

"Walter of course felt as Phelps winemaker he was to be in charge of the operation, but Heitz thought otherwise. He felt that since it was his equipment, *that he* should be in charge. This led to a big struggle that ended up in pulling (powerful) hoses out and power washing each other down right there on the crush pad!"

This "Bordeaux Blend" was *so* successful, it started a myriad of these California versions with unique, proprietary names from other producers. Once again, I was very fortunate to be part of the wholesale team to help launch "Dominus Estate" with Christian Mouiex of Chateau Petrus, and the following year with Director Francis Ford Coppola's "Rubicon", (made by my friend Tony Soter who was the original winemaker at Spottswoode and started his first label Etude and then went up to Oregon to start his namesake winery). Tony would ask me to verify appropriateness the accounts clamoring for his Etude wines, as sort of his spy.

This started a bit of a revolution. Now it seemed like *everyone* was getting in to the act and making their own "Proprietary Blend" crafted with the main five red Bordeaux varietals: Cabernet Sauvignon (a hybrid of Cabernet Franc and Sauvignon Blanc), Cabernet Franc, Merlot, Malbec and Petit Verdot. It became so confusing to Wine Directors, Somms, wine shops and most importantly, the consumer. In 1986, Wine Spectator magazine, decided to eliminate or at least minimize the confusion by running a contest to create a category. You may recall wine lists with "Interesting Reds" or "Other". So here we are, trying to be "pseudo French" and the winner of the contest, some guy from Sacramento, California comes up with "Meritage". One would think, therefore, that it would be pronounced phonetically: "Mere e taj". But, the winners' concept was the fusion of merit and heritage, so the proper pronunciation rhymes with heritage. Insignia started it all! Unintentionally. Ironically, it has never qualified by definition as a Meritage. Wasn't trying to be. Nonetheless, created it. Joseph Phelps was such a visionary, that he was the first one to ever produce a Syrah as a standalone in California, second ever to produce Viognier as a standalone.

Joe grew up on a farm in Colorado, and wanted to insure that raising his family, his four children, Bill, Leslie, Lauri and Lyn had the best meats and produce in the Napa Valley. So he bought the iconic, Oakville Grocery store. Joe was talented in the kitchen too and loved teaching his granddaughter, Allie Phelps who has come into her own as a Chef and hired the Joseph Phelps Culinary team that is creating incredible gastronomic delights to rival that of the French Laundry. Joe's love of wine and food brought him to become good friends with Alice Waters, founding Chef of Chez Panisse in Berkley, credited as being the home of origination of "Farm to Table" cuisine. Alice mentored many a world famous chef, including Jeremiah Towers of Stars, San Francisco. Mr. Phelps had Mr. Schug make her first house wines back in the seventies. As a gesture of their friendship, Ms. Waters designed the original JPV kitchen.

Prior to Joe's passing on April 15, 2015, Robert Parker was invited to come and taste a private retrospective of the entire 40 year vertical of Insignia with just Joe and Bill Phelps. Near the end of this historical event, some film was rolled to capture the essence: Parker holds up a bottle of Insignia and looks straight into the camera.
"Insignia is one of the great wines of the world. And often, it will come out on top!" mic drop. **BOOM!**

*When you go visit Joseph Phelps Vineyards in St. Helena, make sure you see the incredible collection of bottles in the Oval Room. Many of these have been signed, some dated marking the occasion by guests at Joe's legendary dinner parties. Quite heavy in Bordeaux, Burgundy, the Rhone Valley and Germany. When I peruse the room, I realize how fortunate I was to have sold at least three-quarters of these world-class wines in his collection as a wholesaler-not necessarily the same vintages, however!

5

The Eagle has Landed

Never having been to Hawaii before, my fiancé and business partner, Kat, decided that for my 40th birthday that it was about time I experienced true Ohana Aloha. Kat had been to da Islands several times and was gonna show me. Maui was the destination. I had dreamed of Hawaii as a kid living on Sea Island, Georgia and had been surfing there and Jacksonville Beach, Florida prior to that. I wasn't very good, but I liked the vibe-the surfer girls, the smell of newly honed surfboards and Mister Zogs Sex Wax, the salt air of the Atlantic and was diligent "reading" Surfer Magazine. Oh, those pics of California waves had me dreamin' and the ones of Hawaii, oooooh, seemed such a far off idea, but knew some day… some day, I'd get there…

My Mom was of ill health, and my Dad called to say, "Son, if you want to say goodbye to your Mom one last time, now would be the time." So I hung up the phone and called Delta Airlines and booked my flight pronto. I spent a couple of somber days with my bed –ridden Mother, getting closure and reliving some of our favorite moments together. My last words to her were the same ones she would say to me as I would leave to fly back to the University of Denver after Christmas and Spring breaks. "It's ok, you can go now." I knew she needed to hear that from her only son, her baby boy.

So I flew back to San Francisco feeling as best as I could and drove home to Marin. We left the very next day to go to Maui where our marriage license was awaiting us in Lahaina. Since we were going to Hawaii for my birthday, Kat thought we should get maui'd in Maui as our Venture Catalyst business in high tech was booming and we really had no other time to get married. When we called the Westin to see if they could help us with wedding arrangements, the voice on the other end of the phone laughed. "Ha! Do we do weddings?! We are the ninth busiest place in the world for weddings! You need to speak to the Director of Romance." Director of Romance? Wowie! Maui IS the place to get married.

We had beautiful beach side wedding there at the Westin. That morning, I got the call at 5:30 am Hawaiian time from my Dad. "Your Mother is no longer

The Eagle has Landed

suffering and has passed." In my gut I had known. We were 6 time zones later. The sky at sunset was as incredible as I had ever seen and on fire! I knew in my heart that was the only way she could be at our wedding. The next day was my 40th, and we were back on a plane to Sea Island, Georgia. My Dad felt bad and put us up in the Cloister Hotel and had arranged for us to meet the Sommelier there as a wedding present. On the plane, I wrote my Mom's eulogy. It was very cathartic.

When we arrived at Sea Island and were checking into the Cloister, we were tipped off that the Hotel was entirely booked with Merrill Lynch people and that the Glenn Frey Band was going to play for their convention tonight. Furthermore, there was going to be a sound check at the Beach Club at 2:00 pm. Perfect! An hour before our 3:00 appointment with Stephen the Sommelier.

In High School my buddies were really into the band the "Eagles". It seem liked every morning in Art Class, somebody would race to the stereo to put on their Greatest Hits album. I liked 'em all right, but I didn't own any of their records. They were good. I would watch them on The "Midnight Special" or "Don Kirschner's Rock Concert" when they were on. That was a nice introduction to them, but I still didn't buy any of their records, even though I had heard on the radio that Glenn Frey, one of the founding members of the Eagles shared my birthday, November 6th.

My Mom's service was at 11:00 am at St. Francis Church., on Saturday November 7th. It was a beautiful celebration of her life, many memories from her friends, even some great laughs. My family stayed on for some lunch and some tears and then we adjourned, until getting back together for dinner.

Kat and I headed to the Beach Club and started to take a walk on the beach, when we heard the song "The Heat Is On!" Which prompted us to turn around and head back. We moseyed on in to the sound check and there was my birthday buddy singing front and center with his guitar slung around his neck. After rehearsing "You belong to the City" and "Party Town", the band took a break.

I immediately approached Glenn, shook hands and said "Happy Birthday! Well, yesterday."

"How did you know it was my birthday?" Frey asked.

"I've known for a long time that you and I share the same birthday-just 10 years a part." I said.

"So, what areya-60 now?" He quipped and smirked with his sardonic sense of humor and we both had a good laugh.

We listened to "Smuggler's Blues", "Love in the 21st Century" and "Heartache Tonight" and then it was time to go meet Stephen, the 5 Star resort Hotel's Somm. He had 3 wines for us to try. A Joseph Phelps Insignia and Backus and a Cos D'Estournel, all from 1995. The wines were all very young, but had been opened early in the day and showed very well.

Impressive as they were, under the circumstances, I don't recall much more than that. Little did I know twenty years later, I would be working for the Phelps family and selling both the Insignia, California's original Proprietary wine, and one of California's first cult wines, Backus. Yummers!, to say the least.

That night, after my family had dinner and we were done reminiscing on some great old stories of Mom, we all said our goodbyes to each other. Kat and I headed back to the Cloister and on to the Ballroom, where all the Merrill Lynch folks were listening to the Glenn Frey Band. We moved to the back of the room quietly and unpretentiously, not disturbing anybody. In the middle of "Lyin' Eyes" and "Take It Easy" medley, a security guard approached us.

"Let me see your Merrill Lynch badges".

"We're not with Merrill Lynch." I quietly responded.

"Well then you gonna have to leave".

"Please. Come with me and let me explain to you what we have just been through."

After about ten minutes of explaining that were in mourning and the extreme emotional highs and lows of trauma and drama, not to mention jet-lag, we had just experienced.

"I don't give a shit about any of that."

Nice guy.

We reluctantly left and headed to the bar.

The irony of it was that the next morning we're checking out of the Hotel, and so were all 400 Merrill Lynch people. Not only do Glenn and I have the same birthday-but we're doppelgangers, too! I was wearing my aqua blue mirrored, tortoise shell 'gawdawful' sunglasses and some rather psychedelic pants. Several of the conventioneers came up to me and said: "Great show last night, Glenn. Can I have your autograph?"

I chuckled and said: "Thanks, but I'm not Glenn."

"Come on, man. It was a *really* great show! Please, let me have your autograph."

Guess I had the last laugh, and it just reinforced one of my original sayings:

"True enlightenment lies beyond all of Life's ironies and paradoxes."

6

9ers Dude!

Having grown up in Washington D.C. in the '60s, I naturally started as a Redskins fan. They weren't that good at that time with Sonny Jurgensen at QB, but it was always an interesting challenge when the 'Skins would play the Cowboys twice a year. The 'Boys had Roger Staubach at the helm. Seems like Dallas always had the 'skins number. I remember though, a few games where the Redskins were leading by 2 touchdowns midway through the fourth quarter. But alas, inevitably Staubach would find a way to comeback and pull out a victory. Damn it! Not again Roger. Uggh! Once again, not to be avenged… yet.

When I graduated college in 1981, I moved to San Francisco and the Forty-Niners had a new quarterback; a guy named Joe. He was no ordinary Joe, this Montana fella from Notre Dame. Not only would he become a shoe-in for the NFL Hall of Fame, arguably the greatest QB of all time, but he was my avenger with "The Catch" in the 1981 NFC championship game. The 'Niners were down 27 to 21. The last minute throw in desperation to Dwight Clark reaching up high in the corner of the end zone against the Dallas Cowboys defenders, ensured Montana as "Joe Cool" forever-and more than anything, the anguish, the frustration and the angst of 30 years had finally been exonerated-make that *exercised*. I was laughing maniacally to the point of tears, givin' high fives all around the room with my buddies-*oh man! Did <u>that</u> feel good*!

The San Francisco Forty-Niners won 28 to 27 and that moment was the start of the dynasty, winning 4 Super Bowls with Joe Montana. As comedian Robin Williams would say in a somewhat 'street' and somewhat doofy voice "9-ers, Dooooood!"

I met Joe Montana in Redwood City at my largest retail account, K & L. Joe is a huge fan of Caymus Cabernet Sauvignon, and I was the Wine Supervisor that sold Caymus to K & L. Clyde Beffa, one of the owners introduced me to Joe and we talked wine for about 15 minutes or so. This was when Montana had injured his elbow and was out for a season and Steve Young took over as quarterback.

Joe's a helluva nice guy and down to earth. We never talked football, only wine. I don't think I "gushed", even though he was my hero!

He now makes wine himself (as every great retired quarterback should, right?) with the help of Ed Sbragia who crafted so many great Beringer Private Reserve Cabernets, called "Montagia".

VINDICATION!

One of Joe's coaches besides the legendary great Bill Walsh was George Seifert.

He succeeded Walsh as Head Coach, directing the 9ers to winning another Super Bowl. A very reserved man after leaving football, his love of fishing brought him to retiring in Bodega Bay on the Sonoma Coast. One of the most popular eateries was my account the Tides Restaurant. One day I was presenting Nicholson Ranch and Sullivan–Birney wines to Carlo, the owner and wine buyer at the Tides. He asked me to wait for him in the bar. As I entered the bar, there was Seifert quietly seated enjoying a cocktail. "You should be drinking wine", I said winking and holding up a bottle of Chardonnay. "Perhaps I will after this", he winked back.

"What is that you have?" He politely asked. I showed him the bottle and then Carlo waived me over.

"Thanks for ALL those great games!" I said enthusiastically. "It was a great run!"

George nodded and with a very satisfied grin on his face said "Yes. Yes it was".

During the San Francisco Football franchise's dynasty, Carmen Policy was the President who deftly directed the organization for all 5 Super Bowls. He too has his own incredible wine from the Napa Valley "Casa Piena" from his Policy Estates in Yountville.

When you have a Rock Star Winemaker like Thomas Rivers Brown (I knew him when he first got started and was just Thomas Brown) tapering the wine to that specific terroir, you know it's going to be a winner.

The first time I met Carmen was in Yountville where he was manning the table and pouring at Premier Napa downstairs at 1870 Market Place. We had a nice long conversation about wine and football. He invited me to lunch. What a gracious and polite gesture, I thought. The next time I met him a couple of years later, we had a similar conversation and he again invited me to lunch. One of these days I'm going to have to cash in on that rain check.

When I was with Luna Vineyards helping Mike Moon sell the brand and operation, I was asked to pour at the kick off of the new "Pac 12" launch in San Francisco. Driving into the city on Van Ness Street, there was a black guy on the island divider holding a card board sign:

"I lost my African-American Express card and I'm Homeless without it"

I cracked up so hard, I almost drove over the median. "Now <u>that's</u> excellent! *And* Fun-NEE!-this guy deserves some love." So I slowed down long enough to hand over some dough.

I finally arrived at the Pac 12 Headquarters after wading through the pedestrian traffic-as my luck would have it, the San Francisco Giants were at home and the baseball game had just ended, letting out forty-thousand plus rabid fans celebrating the victory at hand. Go Giants!

Forty-Niner great and Hall of Famer Ronnie Lott was there as he was one of the commentators for this televised event. There was a full bar and some great brews there, but Luna was the only winery represented. When I saw Ronnie, I had to make an excuse to meet him of course, as he was a huge part of all this Forty-Niner lore. So, I called him over, shook his hand, introduced myself and said: "I have some *really* nice Reserve Pinot Grigio and Sangiovese over here for you." He looked at me slightly quizzically and replied

"I was told that I should have a "Big Boy' drink."

'Big Boi' drink', I thought to myself, 'Big Boy' drink? Nothing is more sophisticated and displays maturity than a nice glass of wine! And just as I was about to voice that to Mr. Defensive Player of the year, in my mind rolled an all time highlight reel of number 42 smashing into receivers and running backs with a perfectly timed mid- air smack down collision that was seemingly fifteen feet off the ground that inspired awe and ouch!

So, instead, I responded with: "Ok. Well when you *are* ready for some wine, I'll be right here waiting for you."

That night everybody there received a medallion of the newly minted Pack 12 commemorating this historic night. Here's mine:

*Lott and Montana were the backup singers on Huey Lewis' "Hip to be Square"

7

Demystifying the "Flavor Profile"

The Maestro, Andre Tchelistcheff, said "Let the wine talk to you". I totally agree. That's the point I have been trying to drive home for decades. And would further add "and the wine will tell you what to pair with it", if you follow my way of thinking by starting with the wine *first*. Most people tell me that they order the entrée first, then ask for the wine list. That's natural and I suppose "customary". You can certainly pair that way and do a reasonably good job. But I want you to be able to knock the cover off the ball *every time. The logic is, you can't change the wine, as it already has been made, BUT! You, can adapt the food to the wine by breaking down the Flavor Profile.* This is the crux, the core of this book.

How to break down the Flavor Profile of wines.

My philosophy with wines is always to help educate people without intimidating or talking down to them, simultaneously. I think (I hope) I effectively achieve this by setting their expectations from the start, sprinkling in a fun/smartass sense of humor and the tonality in my voice and delivery.

This is my intellectual property and is proprietary information I developed in the mid-'80s. Ultimately it is intended for you to understand how to make complimentary Wine and Food pairings that you know you will knock it out of the park every time. This should also help to demystify describing wines in more detail and to some extent, have a better grasp of how wines age.

Like any conundrum, it is best understood if you break it down into its component parts, right?
So we'll break it down into 3 components:

1) The Fruit Spectrums
2) The Herb and Spice Rack
3) The Miscellaneous category (as in, what else are you getting out of the wine in terms of aromas and tastes that are not fruit, herbs or spices)

When conducting seminars on this topic, I like to get the audience involved

> ## Demystifying the "Flavor Profile"

and make it interactive-it makes it more fun. After all, wine should be fun too, right?

Because wine can be such an intimidating topic, I try to put guests at ease right from the start:

"Welcome everybody! I want to encourage you to ask questions as there are no stupid questions, no dumb answers. So feel comfortable knowing one can never learn it all- I'm still a student after 40 years. And after all, after today, you'll never see these folks again anyway, so what do you care, right?"

Then I ask them to start naming fruits.

We start with the <u>white wine</u> fruit spectrum. You pretty much cannot go wrong with apple and pear-it's always an intelligent response for *any* white wines, so I explain with an apology for the bad pun, "Apple is the core, so we are going to put that right in the middle of an imaginary horizontal line going across the room." And from there, we flesh out all the other fruits they have named and the ones missed like this:

1a) The Fruit Spectrums-White:

More Ripe ←--→ *Higher Acidity*

| Tropical | Melons | Tree | Stone | Citrus |

Guava Banana Pineapple Papaya Mango Kiwi Lychee/ Honeydew Cantaloupe/ Pear Apple/ Apricot Peach Nectarine/ Passion* Nectarine Orange Lime Lemon Grapefruit/Gooseberry

* Note that Passion fruit is not a citrus, but in terms of acidity, it seems to fit here best.

1b) The Fruit Spectrums-Red:

The Red Wine Fruit Spectrum also acts as a bit of a *timeline*. That's partially why I created this, as the number 2 question people always ask me is "How do I know when to drink it?" or "When will this wine be at its peak?" Younger wines are higher in acidity and tend to be reminiscent of more red fruits (on the right); older wines tend to have more of the deeper, darker more "brooding" fruits.

More Ripe ←---→ *Higher Acidity*

Raisins Prunes Dates Fig Olive Black Currant Black Plum Blueberry Bing Cherry Red Cherry Blackberries Red Plum Blood Orange Strawberry Raspberry Pomegranate Red Currant Cranberry

Not only is the Red wine fruit spectrum a "pick list" for what the flavors and aromatics in the wine remind you of, but it acts as a time line too. Going from right (young wine) to left (older wine). This is why I created this concept some 35 years ago, as the number 2 question people always ask me is "When should I drink this?" or "When will it be at its peak?"

For me personally-and you know this is all subjective-the "Sweet Spot" or time to drink is in the middle with the cherries, blueberries, blackberries and plums.

2) The "Herb and Spice Rack"

Having grown up on the East Coast and having been a Wine Educator since 1982 talking about the flavor profile to thousands of audiences, I can get on a pretty good roll and talk *very* fast, to the point of incomprehension.

A few years ago, I was explaining to some guests about the Herb and Spice rack and it went something like this:

"So,abouttheherbandspicerack…"

Demystifying the "Flavor Profile"

"Urban spice rack? Well how is that different from the Country spice rack?"
"Countryspicerack?*Country*spicerack?Whatthehellareyoutalkingabout?"
"Well you're talking about the Urban spice rack."
"Ok, I need to s l o w down." I said, not realizing the reel in my head was making a whole paragraph sound like one word.

The herb and spice rack does not quite lend itself to the same linear connection that the two different fruit spectrums do, but here are the ones I most frequently find reminiscent and as close of a logical order as I can form:

> Peppercorns (black, white, red, green and pink)
> Allspice
> Anise (Star Anise)
> Fennel
> Taragon
> Clove
> Nutmeg
> Cinnamon
> Cardamom
> Cumin
> Ginger
> Cilantro
> Sage
> Oregano
> Bay Leaf
> Mint/
> Basil
> Rosemary
> Lavender
> Violets
> Rose Petals
> Potpourri

I realize the last ones are not technically herbs or spices, but these "florals" are very aromatic and spicy.

Now this is important to note: I love to experiment with exotic spices. Several years ago I was addressing one of my dinner guests about heat inducing spices, like Habanero, Serrano, Cayenne, Chilies and other kinds of peppers. Now I admit that I'm a bit of a lightweight when it comes to heat inducing spices, so your tolerance is probably higher than mine. But the real point here is that the heat knocks out the fruit of the wine and leaves with you just acid and alcohol.

After all, wine is supposed to be a beverage of pleasure, right?!

So just be mindful when using those kinds of spices. As I was addressing this topic one evening to a 'same vintage as me' group of guests, it suddenly dawned on me that my style of cuisine is to have a cacophony going on in the mouth-like Sgt. Peppers' Lonely Hearts Club Band! (No pun intended.) You have all kinds of elements taking place: The excitement is anticipated with the buzz of the audience, and then the drums and bass come in over here and then the electricity of the high note of the electric guitar over there, the surprising immediate impact of the lead singer, next the violins, tympani and other orchestral arrangements, then there are the voices-all coming together for creating a uniqueness and harmony *("All together now!")*

3) The Miscellaneous Category

There is definitely no particular order here and like the 2 categories above, acts as a "pick list" from which to choose.

Often these are Oak Barrel-derived, whether from the Oak itself or the toasting/charring (a caramelization process) of the oak.

This would include:
chocolate, vanilla, caramel, brown sugar, honey, butter, toast, smoke, bacon fat, almonds, coconut, pecans, walnuts, mineral, earth, mushroom, espresso, black tea, tobacco (cedar or cigar box), forest floor, sandlewood, sassafras, cola, beet root, leather, licorice, grass/ herbaceousness, and anything else you might perceive that is not fruit, herbs or spices.

All of these flavors and aromatics remind you of something in your life experience and it is reminiscent of that experience. The wine maker is not putting butter in the Chardonnay, nor chocolate in the Cabernet. Remember in chemistry class the chart of compound structures? All those hexagonals? Well, there are phenolic compounds in wine and it's those phenols and terpenes (for the most part) that remind you of whatever it is that *your* sensory receptors are telling your brain. ("This smell reminds me of…)

But if you have never had a gooseberry or a boysenberry, how would you know?

Demystifying the "Flavor Profile"

Now, these are by no means an entirely exhaustive list on any of these spectrums, but they are fairly comprehensive. Notice that they are all positive in nature, no "rubber hose" or "tennis ball" as described in the movie <u>Somm</u> or "sweat socks", "barnyard", "band aid" or any other derogative descriptor. If you have a wine that you would describe like that-there is only one word for that: *"Garcon!"* –send it back!

So, here's the real lesson here:

By breaking down the Flavor Profile of the wine that you know you want to have that night into those 3 categories or spectrums, you now have your grocery list to see what items are fresh at the market and build the menu around that. Nothing wrong with ordering the entrée and then asking for the wine list to pair, but, here's

The logic: *The wine has already been made, so you can't change it, right? But, you <u>can</u> adapt the food to the wine based on this.*

You'll have guaranteed success of making complimentary wine and food pairings that will WOW! your guests every time.

Reggae Rasta Prawn Pasta con Limon EVOOdo Sauce

There are many variations for this delicious pasta dish, so that we can be sensitive to our vegetarian, pescatarian and gluten free friends as well. Don't think this will work for Vegans however. We'll lay out the whole recipe and you can go back and pull out what does not work for your dietary needs.

Ingredients:
- Angel hair or Spaghetti shape organic pasta (gluten free, if possible) 500 grams (17.60 ounce or thereabout)
- 1 pound 21-25 shrimp (or larger) tail-on (optional) peeled and deveined
- 3-4 large and soft Meyer Lemons enough to squeeze juice to make 2/3 cup
- 1/3 cup Extra Virgin Olive Oil (EVOO)
- 1/3 pound bacon lardons or sun-dried tomatoes
- 1 bunch fresh basil
- ½ cup Parmesan or Pecorino cheese flakes
- 1/3 cup Kalamata olives
- Teaspoon red chili pepper flakes (optional)
- 1 small Cantaloupe cut in ½ inch chunks (you may end up using only half this-don't worry- whaddaya doin' for breakfast tomorah?)
- <u>Herbs:</u> a generous pinch each of dried oregano, sage, thyme, savory, cannabis flowers (optional, and <u>only</u> if legal where you live) and marjoram

For the Pasta:
» Pour 2 quarts of water in a large boiling pot. Add a pinch of salt to expedite boiling process. Add a table spoon of EVOO for texture and non-stick starchiness.
» Once water comes to a rolling boil,
» Add pasta and cook for 10-11 minutes, until "al dente".
» Keep some of the pasta water (about 1/3 cup) for mixing the sauce.

Making the Lardons:
» In a large skillet, cook bacon lardons (cut in half inch cubes) until crispy-caution!
» Try not to break up lardons when turning. You'll love the interplay between the salty lardons and sweet ripeness of the melon.
» Retain the bacon fat to sauté' prawns. Sauté' prawns in same skillet, about a

minute to a minute and a half on each side, flipping with tongs, remove from skillet.

The "EVOOdo" Sauce:
- In a large mixing bowl, pour in saved hot pasta water.
- Add cheese flakes and stir, until creamy.
- Add herbs, stirring until herbs blend with consistency.
- Immediately add EVOO and lemon juice, stirring constantly until consistent.
- Add pasta and stir thoroughly.
- Place sauced pasta into four individual bowls.
- Add additional cheese if so desired.
- Top with lardons, olives, sun dried tomatoes, basil.
- Arrange prawns neatly on top and serve pronto!
- Stick a cannabis leaf on top of each plate if so desired.

Note: *Makes a great vegetarian dish without prawns and substituting sundried tomatoes for the bacon lardons. (if cheese is also not an option, substitute sautéed pine nuts.)

** Makes a great pescatarian dish substituting sundried tomatoes for the bacon lardons.

Pair with a rich style (partially oaked) of Pinot Grigio or lighter style Sangiovese (100%, or minimal blend of Cabernet Sauvignon, Merlot and/or Syrah).

A rich style of Pinot Grigio will have enough "heft" to take on the rich flavors of the bacon fat and/or tomatoes and olives and add a wonderful fruitiness in addition to the lemony EVOOdo sauce and Cantaloupe pieces.

A Sangiovese will add a velvety texture to the sauce and will have tamer tannins than a Super Tuscan style while still standing up to the bold flavors.

"Cin Cin!"

Classic Classical Whole Roasted Chicken Provencal

Ingredients:
- 1 whole chicken (Petaluma Farms, preferably)
- 1/8 cup granulated garlic or 3 cloves fresh Gilroy garlic
- 1/8 cup Herbs du Provence
- 1 Meyer lemon
- 4-6 sprigs fresh Rosemary
- Hawaiian Coral Sea Salt shaker

Instructions:
- Preheat oven to 425 degrees.
- Clean bird thoroughly, washing outside skin and patting dry. Note: if using garlic powder, leave skin slightly wet for garlic crystals to adhere. Clean out cavity and remove any organs if present.
- Cut lemon into slices, quarter size. Stuff slices inside cavity, slightly squeezing juice inside.
- Stuff Rosemary sprigs into cavity.
- Place chicken in Pyrex dish breast side up.
- Rub fresh garlic all over skin of bird or sprinkle granulated garlic cover entire exposed skin.
- Sprinkle Herbs du Provence thoroughly cover entire exposed skin.
- Place in oven on middle rack for 30 minutes and turn Pyrex dish around for even cooking.
- Turn oven down to 400 degrees for 10 minutes, or until leg starts to loosen from body.
- Pull chicken out of oven and let stand for 10 minutes on top of stove, crack Sea Salt all around and cut chicken into halves. Serve with curried couscous.
- Pair with moderately oaked Carneros Chardonnay. The pear and green apple notes will make the succulence of the chicken all the more juicy, while the lemon zest notes will pick up the aromatics of the Meyer lemon and the fennel in the Herbs du Provence will make a nice (French) accent to the Star Anise/licorice in the finish of the Chardonnay. If you add a side of Curried Cous-Cous, the curry spice will pick up the cedar from the oak barrel.

Dish ain't no Funky Chicken!

Shakin' Seared Sea Scallop Shuffle

(Pan Seared Sea Scallops with Avocado 'scallops' and Strawberry Hearts)

Ingredients:
- 6 Large Sea Scallops (pink color is best)
- 2 tablespoons salted butter
- 2 large ripe Haas Avocadoes
- 1 pint fresh strawberries
- Tablespoon granulated garlic

Instructions:
» Slice strawberries into quarters vertically to make "hearts". Place all around

» inner and outer edges of a clear or white side plate, leaving room in center for the Sea Scallops.
» Half the avocados and remove pit. Take a tablespoon and scoop out spoonfuls ("scallops") of avocado and place on plate alternating between strawberry hearts.
» In a small pan, melt butter on high heat until butter starts to brown (about 20 seconds)
» Immediately add garlic and swirl around pan
» Immediately place sea scallops (wider side down) into pan and sear for two minutes.
» Turn off burner and flip scallops over for two minutes. Remove immediately and place 3 scallops in center of a white or clear glass plate. Drizzle remaining sauce, if any, over the bivalves only.
» Serve pronto! Pair with your favorite dry Rose' that accentuates notes of strawberry, watermelon and raspberry. (I personally prefer a Rose' of Pinot Noir.) If you don't like Rose's, try with a barrel fermented Napa Sauvignon Blanc instead and squeeze the juice of 2 Passion Fruits on top of the scallops just prior to serving.

This is a great First course and an aphrodisiac and therefore only serves 2-up to you…

__Just sayin'…__

Dancin' Duck Breasts confit with Grand Marnier infused cherries and Asian 5 spice

Ingredients:
- 4 large Duck Breasts
- 1 cup dehydrated Bing cherries (do NOT use sour cherries!)
- 1 and ½ -2 ounces Grand Marnier
- 2 teaspoons Asian (Chinese) Five Spice (in the ethnic isle)

Instructions:
» Place Bing cherries in a small to medium size bowl, drizzle Grand Marnier over the top of fruit and toss, several times to coat. (can be made up to 4 hours in advance)

» Pre-heat skillet on medium high for 1 minute, 15 seconds.

» Pan sear duck breasts, skin side down in a large skillet for about 12 to 15 minutes on medium to medium high heat, or until mostly firm (caution: will spatter).

» Turn heat down to medium, and flip breasts over, carefully, for 5 minutes. Let the fat render for 5 more minutes. Toss cherries once more and then sprinkle Chinese Five spice and toss to evenly coat the berries.

» Remove breasts from pan to a cutting board and lightly pat with a paper towel.

» Keep skin side up and cut breasts in half (if desired) and generously sprinkle cherry mixture on top, falling off the sides.

» Accompany with Wild rice, garlic mashed potatoes or mushroom risotto (see recipe). Serves 4

Pair with Russian River or Santa Lucia Pinot Noir. The luscious deep fruit of these Pinots will make the whole dish succulent! The Bing cherries are always a great match with these wines-the GM just makes the whole gastronomic experience sparkle and the spices take it over the top.

Soulfulfilling Creamy Wild Mushroom Risotto

Ingredients:

- 4 garlic cloves, diced
- 1 large white onion, diced
- ½ cup, olive oil (preferably EVOO)
- 4 tablespoons unsalted butter
- 2 cups Arborio rice
- 8 ounces Chardonnay (or other dry white wine)
- 4 cups chicken broth, divided
- 1 cup chicken stock
- 2 cups various sliced wild mushrooms (Baby Portabella, Trumpet, Oyster, Hen of the Wood, Morel)
- 1 cup Pecorino, Parmesan or Provolone (combine all 3 if possible, for best results)
- Sea Salt to taste.

Instructions:

» In a large skillet, combine olive oil, garlic and onions and sauté for 4 minutes on medium.
» Add the rice and cook for 3 minutes, stirring well (best not to leave stove at this point).
» Add the Chardonnay to mixture and cook until liquid has evaporated.
» Add chicken stock, one cup at a time, stirring frequently until evaporated.
» Add chicken stock and wild mushrooms. Cook until rice is 'al dente' and creamy.
» Stir in the butter and ½ of the cheeses until blended (about 20 seconds)
» Sprinkle reaming cheese, crack sea salt and add Italian parsley if desired. Serve immediately with: Sangiovese or Super Tuscan Style Cal/Ital Buon appetitio!

"Jammin' Slammin' Salmon"

Grilled Salmon with Heirloom Tomato Rainbow Peppercorn Cream Sauce

Four 8 ounce Salmon fillets-no tails! (Any kind of Salmon works, I particularly like King or anything wild caught. In a pinch, farm raised, skin-on will do.)

INGREDIENTS:
- 4-6 medium to large Heirloom Tomatoes (mix up the colors, the more unusual looking, the better).
- ½ cup heavy cream or half and half. (Come on! You exercise, *anyway*, RIGHT??!)
- 1/8 cup of Rainbow color peppercorns (red, green, pink, black and white).

Instructions:

» Grill Salmon steaks directly on the barbeque or on a cedar plank. The idea here for pairing is a wine with some oak on it. If fillets are placed directly on the grill, the char lines will make a nice compliment to the toasting of the oak barrels. For a wine that has been fermented and/or aged in newer oak barrels, that's where the cedar plank comes in to play. If using a cedar plank, make sure you soak the planks in water or wine for at least a couple of hours. White wine is preferred, but red is fine too. This way the fish won't stick. <u>Always best to place the skin side down for either way of grilling.</u> If directly on the grill, cook each side 6-8 minutes, depending on the thickness of the fish and how hot the grill is. On the cedar plank, do NOT turn over, but let cook for 14 minutes or until medium rare. (Remember proteins continue to cook off the grill.)

» Preheat oven to 275 degrees, once charcoals are lit.

» Slice the Heirlooms in half, horizontally and place on medium size baking sheet, skin side down for 9 minutes.

» On the stove, place a medium size pan and set to medium heat, pour in cream.

Add peppercorns. Swirl sauce every 10 seconds for two and half minutes. Turn off heat and let simmer for 2 minutes, just before removing tomatoes from oven. Place tomato halves on individual plates; make it colorful, leaving the center of the plate for the fish. Drizzle peppercorn cream sauce over tomatoes.
» Place Salmon on middle of plate and serve immediately.

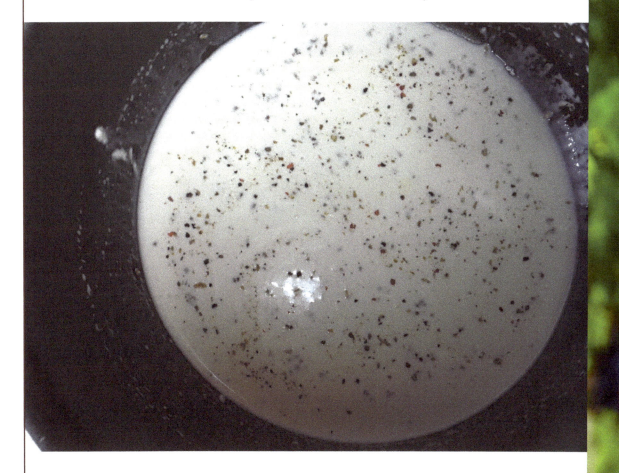

» Pair with a lighter style of Sonoma Zinfandel, Barbera, Merlot or an oaked Chardonnay or Sauvignon Blanc: the acidity in the tomatoes will make any of these wines "pop" all the more!

<u>Zinfandel</u> *will pull out the fruit of the toms and its natural berry flavor and its inherent spice of black pepper will bode well with the sauce.*

<u>Merlot</u> *will add a richness to the oiliness of the fish and its blueberry flavors will complement the tomatoes.*

<u>Barbera's</u> *high acidity will cancel out the acidity of the tomatoes, giving lift to*

the wines' blueberry fruit, pushing it forward and adding additional zing and sweetness to the cream sauce.

Chardonnay will add a subtle nuttiness and complexity and its acidity will cut through the cream sauce and lighten up the dish.

Sauvignon Blanc will perk up the sauce with its acidity and cancel out the acidity of the tomatoes while the natural herbal component will play off nicely with the green peppercorns.

You might want to add a side of the simplest version of the Reaggae Rasta Pasta and sauce.

"We jammin'!"-Bob Marley

Prescient Pear and Punk Pomegranate Salad

Ingredients:
- 2 ripe Bartlett or Anjou pears, sliced thinly
- 1 Pomegranate, sliced in half, remove arils (seeds) by bending membrane and releasing onto pear slices
- 3-4 ounces, bleu or goat cheese; add in chunks

Instructions:
» Toss together

So simple and succulent! 'Pears' with just about any dish. As for wine, try with a Grenache, Garnacha Rose or fruity Mouvedre.

Texas Two-Step Terrific Teriyaki Tri Tip

Ingredients:
- 3-4 pound whole Tri Tip, fat cap and silver skin removed

Marinade:
- 10 ounces of red wine
- 1/3 cup Kikkoman Soy Sauce
- 1/3 cup Balsamic Vinegar
- 5 tablespoons granulated garlic
- 3 tablespoons powdered ginger
- 1 tablespoon dry mustard

Instructions:
» Combine all above ingredients into a medium mixing bowl, marinating Pyrex dish or Tupperware, evenly distributing and integrating.
» Add Tri Tip Steak and submerge into marinade, cover and refrigerate for 4 hours, then turn over to the other side for 4 hours. (Can sit overnight if desired.)
» Light a charcoal fire on the grill and remove meat from marinade and discard marinade. Place Tri Tip on the grill, adding vine canes, mesquite or apple wood chips directly on to the charcoals and cook to your desired specifications I prefer medium rare.
» Cut the meat on the bias in 1/8 inch slices, retaining au jus.
» This terrific cut of steak will blossom with a glass of a young Napa Valley Cabernet Sauvignon or Bordeaux blend. It's that simple. 'Nuff said.

"What contemptible scoundrel stole the cork from my lunch?"
-W.C. Fields

Rhythm and Blues Barbeque Baby back Ribs

Babyback Ribs with "Double Secret" Dry Rub and Boysenberry Hoisin Dipping Sauce

Ingredients:
- A) 2-3 Extra Meaty Baby Back Rib Racks
- B) "Double Secret" Dry Rub
- C) Boysenberry Hosin Sauce

Double Secret* Dry Rub
In a medium size bowl, hand toss:
- 4 tablespoons garlic powder
- 2 tablespoons dry mustard
- 2 teaspoons granulated ginger
- 2 teaspoons cinnamon
- 4 tablespoons granulated cumin or toasted cumin seeds
- 4 tablespoons "Mrs. Dash"
- 3 teaspoons onion powder
- 1/4 cup brown sugar
- 1 teaspoon Ancho Chili powder
- 2 tablespoons smoked paprika
- 4 tablespoons fresh coarsely ground black peppercorns

Instructions:
» Mix well-if you think you're done toss a few more times. (Can be made a day in advance)

BOYSENBERRY HOISIN SAUCE

INGREDIENTS:
- 4 jars 8.5 ounce Lee Kum Kee Hoisin Sauce (or your preferred brand)
- 2 pints of fresh Boysenberries (or other fresh blackberries), the juicier, the mo' bettah!
- Combine all ingredients in a large, pretty serving bowl and mash berries with a fork and mix to desired consistency. I like it a bit chunky. (Can refrigerate up to 24 hours before, but fresher, *is* better.)

INSTRUCTIONS:
» Light a grill with mesquite charcoals, Applewood or grapevine canes are best, if possible.
» Place racks on grill bone side down, meat side up for 30 minutes.

» Turn racks over and place meat side down for 10 minutes or until desired crispiness.
» Pull Babybacks off grill and let rest for 10 minutes on cutting board and generously sprinkle sea salt (Himilayan pink if ya got it).
» With a butcher knife, cut individual bones on cutting board and transfer to platter.

I like the dipping sauce on the side, but if you prefer, drizzle over the top of the ribs.

Pair with a Dry Creek Valley Zinfandel, Paso Robles Petite Sirah or Sierra Foothills Tempranillo.

Zinfandel and **Petite Sirah** have a natural affinity for pork as the tannins are soft enough but still provide some umph, while the bramble berry fruit adds to the succulence and the inherent black pepper spice works so well with the "Double Secret" dry rub. **Tempranillo** has a similar affect, but even softer warm berry tones and minerality playing off the spicy notes.

"Flava Ya Savor"

Yam Frites Shakin' with Asian 5 spice

(perfect with the Babyback Ribs)

Ingredients:
- 2-3 medium to large Yams or Sweet Potatoes
- 2 tablespoons (Asian) Chinese 5 Spice (in your Grocers' Ethnic aisle or Spice rack-not the "Country" Spice rack! (LOL) or cinnamon, if you prefer.
- ¼ cup of Brown Sugar
- 1/3 cup EVOO (Extra Virgin Olive Oil)
- Sea Salt Shaker

Instructions:
- Thoroughly rinse off potatoes in cold water. Pad dry.
- Pre heat oven to 425 degrees.
- Cut potatoes in half, then cut into wedges and then into fries.
- Hand toss raw fries in a large mixing bowl with EVOO, *thoroughly* coating with oil. Add extra, if need be. Crack Sea Salt to desirability. Toss again.
- Place frites onto large baking sheet, arranging bigger slices in the middle, smaller slices on the outer fringe of baking sheet for more even cooking.
- Before placing raw fries into oven, shake and sprinkle 5 spice and brown sugar onto the fries.
- Bake for 20 minutes. Turn baking sheet 180 degrees around to ensure even browning and let bake for 10 minutes more, checking to make sure thin frites don't burn. Serve immediately. Best paired with Zinfandel or Mouvedre.

Zinfandel with its natural spice component will play nicely with the 5 spices and push forward the bramble fruit and inherent sweetness of the potato and brown sugah.

Mouvedre will accent the darker "bass" notes of nutmeg, clove, and star anise adding dimension.

"Whole Lotta Shakin' Going On!"-Jerry Lee Lewis

Struttin Leg o' Lamb with Rosemary Dijon Mustard Crust and Wild Mushrooms

Ingredients:
- 16-20 ounce New Zealand Lamb Leg, deboned and butterflied
- 10-12 sprigs Fresh Rosemary
- 12 ounce jar Dijon Mustard (not whole grain)
- Half pound of Fresh Wild Mushrooms (Shitakes, Chanterelles, Morels, Hen of the Woods, etc.)
- 2 tablespoons unsalted butter
- Six 6 inch canes (from vine canopy pruning's-if not available, apple wood or mesquite will do nicely)

Instructions:
- Light a charcoal fire on the grill.
- Wash lamb leg thoroughly, pad dry and butterfly.
- Slather lamb with Dijon Mustard and coat entirely.
- Generously sprinkle with destemmed rosemary.
- Drop canes, apple wood or mesquite chips directly on charcoals.
- Immediately place lamb leg on grill, butterflied side down for about 25 minutes-careful not to scorch your eyebrows! Not that that has ever happened to me ; -)
- Sautee wild mushrooms in pan-BUT! Only half way (about 7 minutes), as they will be finished off on the grill.*
- Temporarily take lamb leg off grill, flip over and reserve.
- *Place partially sautéed mushrooms into open cavity of leg and wrap leg back up with string or pins to seal in mushrooms and juices.
- Crack coarse black peppercorns and sea salt onto leg.
- Place back on grill for another 20-25 minutes, depending on desired doneness.
- (I highly suggest medium rare to medium.)
- Take lamb off grill, let rest for 10 minutes and slice into 1/8 inch thick pieces.
- Reserve au jus to spoon back over pieces upon platting.
- Serve with roasted small New potatoes* or smashed Fingerlings, or the Mushroom Risotto.

A Napa Howell Mountain **Merlot**, Stag's Leap District **Cabernet Sauvignon** or Mount Veeder **Malbec**. Any of these Napa mountain grown, Bordeaux varietals will stand up to the intensity of the char and the natural gaminess of the lamb and au jus, while their mineral notes will accentuate the earthiness of the wild mush

"I enjoy a glass of wine each night for its health benefits.
The other glasses are for my witty comebacks and my flawless dance moves."
— Unknown

Rockin' Moroccan Glazed Carrots with Pine Nuts and Olives

Ingredients:

- 8-12 Fresh Carrots (Skinny to medium width, about 8 -10 inches long)
- 1/3 cup Pinenuts
- ½ cup whole, pitted Kalamata Olives
- 2-3 tablespoons whole Coriander seeds
- 2 tablespoons Brown Sugar
- 1/8 cup Extra Virgin Olive Oil
- Tablespoon unsalted Butter
- Tablespoon Extra Virgin Olive Oil
- For the Middle Eastern Spices:
- 2 Tablespoons ground Cinnamon
- 2 Tablepoons ground Cardamom
- Teaspoon ground Cumin
- Teaspoon Tumeric

Instructions:

» In a large skillet (large enough for the carrots to sit neatly and flatly) sauté Pinenuts in the butter and the tablespoon of EVOO on medium low heat until golden brown (about 4-6 minutes; stir constantly so as not to burn) remove from skillet and set aside. Do NOT clean skillet.

» While sautéing Pinenuts, in a separate small skillet, toast Coriander seeds on low heat and monitor CONSTANTLY, turning from time to time until fragrant (about 4-5 minutes). Remove from heat and set aside.

» Wash carrots leaving peel on, discard any green tops.

» Place carrots in pan that was used for pinenuts, alternating every other fat ends and skinny ends and add the 1/8 cup of EVOO and roll the vegetables in the oil until coated. Generously sprinkle the carrots with the Middle Eastern spices. (You may want to mix these ingredients together ahead of time.)

» On high heat, blister the carrots for 20 minutes.

» With tongs, flip carrots over to opposite side and blister for 5 more minutes.

» Turn down to medium and roll veggies in the skillet. Sprinkle brown sugar and add olives on top of carrots for 10 more minutes and then let simmer, adding back pine nuts. Plate up and sprinkle toasted Coriander seeds on top. Serve with the Lamb dish. If you're a Vegetarian, this makes a great meal by itself, loaded with flavors and textures, the Pinenuts give a nice richness to the dish and some crunch along with the pop and fragrance of the coriander seeds. Plenty of spice to play off the sweetness of the caramelized carrots and brown sugar, and the salty notes from the Kalamatas. Pair this with a dry Chenin Blanc or Gewürztraminer from Mendocino, or a San Luis Obispo Malbec.

Bebop Beat Beets

"Dance to your own Beat, Beets!"

Ingredients:
- 8-12 Golden and/or Red Beets (half and half is purty!)
- 4 ounces Laura Chenel Goat Cheese (or your fav)
- Whole pomegranate (optional)
- 5 Large Basil Leaves, hand torn length wise into approximately 1 inch strips
- Teaspoon smoked Paprika
- Sea Salt and Coarse cracked Black Pepper to taste

Instructions:
- Place beets (peeled and cut into 1-inch pieces) in a large pot of boiling salted water. Reduce heat to a simmer and cook until beets are tender when pierced with a knife, 15 to 20 minutes; drain. Let cool in frig for ½ hour, in a large serving bowl.
- Remove pomegranate perils from membrane and place in separate bowl
- Remove beets from frig and toss beets in bowl with remaining beet juice.
- Top with pomegranate perils.
- *n.b. (If you wanna 'cheat', buy pre-peeled and cooked "Love Beets" brand- Hoodoouluv ?)
- Add salt and peppah. Toss.
- Pinch or squeeze cheese (each about a finger nails worth) onto beets, distributing evenly. Do NOT toss-it's not a pretty sight!
- Sprinkle smoked Paprika onto goat cheese.
- Keep covered and refrigerated until ready to use. (Up to an hour.)
- Add Basil strips just beet4 serving.

Pair these delectable gems with a **Sonoma Coast or Anderson Valley Pinot Noir**, as the deep flavors of these AVA ("American Viticultural Area") wines will pull out the natural beet root and the earthiness of the Pinot fruit grown here. The slight smokiness of the Paprika will make a nice enhancement to the Oak without offing too much heat. The basil will give a freshness and new dimension of contrast.

This veggie dish will make a nice balancing act to any of the entrees or other vegetable dishes in this book. Additionally, try a **Pinot Noir** from Santa Rita Hills that will match Beet Root flavors, a Paso Robles **Petite Sirah** with all its earthiness and tannic grip to emphasize the root vegetables' origins or a well oaked **Chardonnay** from San Luis Opisbo's Edna Valley that will complement the goat and the smoked paprika, along with the wine's star anise finish that will set off the licorice note of the basil.

Fabuloso!

Whole Roasted Sashaying Sea Bass

Ingredients:

- 2 Whole Sea Bass, 2 pounds each (filleted, head and tail intact)
- 1 Red Bell Pepper
- 1 Yellow Bell Pepper
- ½ Bunch Fresh Cilantro
- 1 Blade Lemongrass, minced
- ½ cup Fresh Shitake Mushrooms
- 1 and ½ Tablespoons Teriyaki (Soy Vay Brand)
- 1 tablespoon toasted Sesame seeds
- 2 tablespoons Fresh Ginger root, finely minced
- 1 large Fresh Garlic clove, finely minced
- 2 Tablespoons Sea Salt

Instructions:

- Pre heat oven to 400 degrees
- Toss Shitakes in teriyaki.
- Dice peppers into 1/8th inch diamond shapes
- Place fish in Pyrex dish (preferred) or on baking sheet with parchment paper or aluminum foil
- Neatly arrange and alternate peppers, mushrooms and cilantro in cavity of fish-make it pretty!
- Sprinkle minced ginger, garlic and lemongrass on top of the above ingredients
- Crack or sprinkle sea salt on skin with even distribution (upside only is fine)
- Bake for 30 minutes
- Remove from oven and cover loosely with aluminum foil and let steam for no more than 10 minutes, or serve immediately.

Pair with a Willamette Valley Pinot Noir or a crisp Viognier. (if serving a Viognier, don't include the mushrooms.)

Delicious Fishness!

Curried Coconut Lemon Cucumbers

"Cukes with a little nuke"
Very simple and Ahhh, *refreshing!*

Ingredients:
- 3 medium size Lemon Cucumbers
- 1/3 cup chilled Coconut milk
- Teaspoon red curry paste
- Tablespoon fresh Gilroy garlic, minced
- 2-3 sprigs Cilantro (optional)
- 2-3 large Basil leaves (optional)

Instructions:
- In a decorative serving bowl, pour in Coconut milk.
- With a fork, add curry paste into milk and blend evenly and thoroughly.
- Slice Cucumbers into 1/8 inch rounds and place in the bowl to soak up the Coconut Curry Milk for 5 minutes.
- Top cukes with ginger and toss thoroughly.
- Slice Basil into strips and pull Cilantro pieces apart for garnish topping, if desired.

This is fantastic with a **Viognier!** The floral notes of Star Jasmine, honeysuckle and citrus blossom of the **Viognier** bode well for the fragrance of the coconut, garlic and curry spices (and a lil' kick!), while the pear and mandarin orange flavors of the wine will balance the richness of the milk. The garni adds additional herbal aromatics and nuance.

Perfect companion for the "Sashaying Seabass"
"Skaal Y'all!"

Kickin' Killer Krab Kakes

Ingredients:
- Whole Dungeness Crab freshly cooked (can be a day prior)-each one should be enough meat for 2 people. (roughly 8-10 ounces)
- 2 large eggs
- Kup Italian herbed Panko krumbs
- Tablespoon smoked paprika and/or teaspoon Kayenne pepper
- Kup kooked mash potatoes, chilled
- 1 and ½ tablespoons EVOO (enough to coat pan)
- Mango Tango Salsa Salsa! (recipe on next page)

Instructions:
- Krack, Klean and pull crabmeat out of the shell, legs and claws and place in separate mixing bowl. Cover tightly and refrigerate (no more than 2 hours) until ready to use.
- *If adding parika and/or Kayenne, in a salad or small mixing bowl hand toss with bread krumbs, mixing thoroughly.
- Sprinkle mixture generously on to a dinner plate.
- Scoop out a handful (half kup) of mashed potatoes.
- Krack egg onto potato. Mold and fold egg into mashers thoroughly with your hands, shaping the Kake. This will help bind it together.
- Grab a good size handful of the Krab, and fold it into the potatokake.
- Roll krabpotatokake on to the panko plate, until thoroughly coated.
- Flaten out to a an even 1/2 -1/3 inch thickness.
- When ready to kook, evenly coat a large skillet with the EVOO, ensuring the sides of the pan have been dressed as well.
- Place pan on burner on high heat for one minute.
- Add krabpotaokakes into pan and reduce heat to medium for 4 minutes.
- Flip kakes over and cook for 3 more minutes or to desired doneness.
- Remove from skillet and arrange neatly on plates immediately.
- Spoon top with Mango Tango Salsa Salsa
- You may want to add the Hip-Hop Jicama slaw if for an entrée.

A crisp refreshing white is in order here:

Sauvignon Blanc, with its natural herbaceuosness will pick up the Italian herbs very nicely and its acidity will balance out the acidity in the salsa as well as the citrus will counterbalance the tropical fruit of the mango.

Albarino, with its richness, will be a nice compliment to the viscosity of the potato and the bread crumbs and be a nice counter to the mango.

A **Riesling** low in alcohol will be especially brilliant to counter the heat if using the Cayenne pepper, while the natural apple and apricot of the wine will play of the tropical side of the salsa.

PROST!

Mango Tango Salsa Salsa!
(makes ya wanna dance!)

This is fantastically refreshing for grilled Mahi Mahi fish tacos in a crunchy shell or grilled fresh Hawaiin, wild caught Swordfish steaks. I also recommend my green olive tapenade instead (see recipe) for the Swordfish. Make sure your Fishmonger cuts the blood portion out. And with my Kickin' Killer Krab Kakes-*OOH-La-La!*

Ingredients:
- 3 <u>ripe</u> Mangos, peeled completely and diced
- 1 bunch Cilantro, chopped, leave some stem
- 2 red bell peppers (these are sweet, not hot), diced or minced
- 1 smoked Italian red onion or raw if you want some heat, diced or minced
- 2 thin skinned limes
- 1 thin skinned Eureka lemon

Preparation:
» Toss mangoes, peppers and onion together.
» Add cilantro, toss some more –it should look beautiful to you with its array of alternating colors.
» Lastly squeeze limes and lemon, toss once more (lively up yourself!)

For Ceviche Cha Cha Cha-
- 12 ounces of raw halibut, snapper, rock shrimp (Rock on!), Ahi tuna, Bay scallops, salmon or crab (or make your fav combo) diced in chunks-chunky, not funky.
» Place seafood in nonreactive bowl and squeeze ½ cup fresh squeezed lemon juice (save rind for garnish twist), and let sit for 20-30 minutes, tossing every 5 minutes to thoroughly "cook" the fish and the raw onion. The acidity in the citrus will do this for you. Toss one more time and add mango salsa, mixing thoroughly.
» Place 4 ounces of the mixture in a Martini glass, garnish with lemon peel twist and top with cilantro garni. Exquisite!

Serve the ceviche with a crisp (unoaked) **Sauvignon Blanc** for all the brightness to come forward and overcoming, but not overpowering the fish. The herbal notes ("grassy") of the SB will complement the earthiness of the cilantro. The high acidity in the wine will also cancel out the acidity in the lemon and lime juice. Add blue corn tortilla chips if ya like, or use demi-tasse spoons. You'll want to reach to the bottom of this one!

"You're a really good dancer"-Alcohol

Succulent Swingin' Swordfish

Simply grill <u>fresh</u> Swordfish steaks (1 inch thick) on the Barbie for 5-6 minutes, turning 90 degrees for perfect grill marks, for another 2-3 minutes and flip over for 2 more-do not overcook! Top with "Mango Tango Salsa Salsa" and pair with **Sauvignon Blanc** (see recipe and explanation of wine pairing), or a fruity, somewhat buttery **Chardonnay** or rich **Albarino** that will make a nice foil to the richness of the sweet Mango fruit and stand up to the meaty fish or swing it into entirely different directions by topping with my "Tap Dancin' Tapenades". If you go with the green olive one, pair with **Sauvignon Blanc** or **Gruner Veltiner** to pull out the herbal flavors in the wine, olive fruit and toasted coriander seeds. If you choose the black olive one, a Napa **Merlot** or Sonoma **Cabernet Sauvignon** with some age on it will have the heft to stand up to the bold flavors of the tapenade, but the tannins will be in check to not overpower yet stand up to the Sword steak. The pyrazines in these wines will play nicely with the herbal aspects of the toasted fennel seeds.

"Salud!"

Tap Dancin' with Tapenades

Black Olive Tapenade
- 8 ounces Oil-cured Black or Kalamata olives (or combo)
- 2 tablespoons of caper berries
- 2 Anchovy fillets (or sub a tablespoon of Miso)
- 2 garlic gloves, minced
- Tablespoon Fennel seeds (toasted)
- Teaspoon of ground Madagascar cinnamon
- Tablespoon of brown sugar
- Tablespoon Dijon mustard
- Tablespoon Red wine (like Zinfandel)
- 2 tablespoons EVOO

Instructions:
» In a small skillet, toast fennel seeds on medium heat for about 3 minutes or until fragrant-*do not leave the stove until done, constantly stirring as not to burn.* Turn off heat and let sit.

» In a food processor, blend olives, Anchovies, capers, garlic, mustard, brown sugah, cinnamon and wine. Should make a fine paste. Add olive oil and fennel, blend for 45 seconds. Spoon into Mason jar to preserve or serve fresh with seeded flatbread crackers, stuff into a celery stick with Gorgonzola cheese, or top on Swordfish steaks.

This is a perfect companion for a young Napa **Cabernet Sauvignon**, **Bordeaux** blend or California GSM (**Grenache, Syrah and Mouvedre**).

Green Olive Tapenade

Ingredients:
- 8 ounces Large Spanish Queen green olives (remove pimentos)
- 2 tablespoons of caper berries
- 2 Anchovy fillets (or sub a tablespoon of chopped Sun-Dried tomatoes)
- 2 garlic gloves, minced
- Tablespoon Coriander seeds (toasted)
- Teaspoon of ground Madagascar cinnamon
- Tablespoon of brown sugar
- Tablespoon dried herbs (Thyme, Rosemary and/or Marjoram)
- Tablespoon White wine (like Sauvignon Blanc)
- 2 tablespoons EVOO

Instructions:
» In a small skillet, toast Coriander seeds on medium heat for about 3 minutes or until fragrant-*do not leave the stove until done, constantly stirring as not to burn.* Turn off heat and let sit.

» In a food processor, blend olives, Anchovies, capers, garlic, brown sugah, cinnamon and wine. Should make a fine paste. Add olive oil and Coriander, blend for 45 seconds. Spoon into Mason jar to preserve or serve fresh with seeded flatbread crackers with melted Brie or St. Andre' cheese, or top on "Swingin' Swordfish steaks". You might also try with the "Gangstah Double Cut Brined Pork Chop".

This is a perfect companion for an herbaceous Paso Robles **Merlot** or **Bordeaux** blend or Russian River **Sauvignon Blanc**.

Sandrew's Sufferin' Summer Succotash

If I had to choose only one favorite cartoon character from the Looney Tunes franchise, it would have to be Daffy Duck. I loved his creative genius and humorous perspective on life, even though it often backfired on him-maybe that's why I can relate to him so much. I know, I know, it was Sylvester the Cat who said "thufferin' thucatash", but both Thylvester and Daffy shared a lisp.

Ingredients:
- 3 Large Ears of fresh corn (preferably white, but yellow will do), shucked.
- 2-3 large just ripe Nectarines (preferably white, but yellow will do and so will peaches, if nectarines are not available). Note: It's the higher acidity that you are looking for, as the sweetness will be derived as much from the creaminess of the freshly shucked corn.
- 1/2 cup large Spanish Queen green olives with pimento intact.

INSTRUCTIONS:

- Steam corn in microwave for 3 minutes, flip over and steam for 1 minute more, let cool.
- Meanwhile, chop olives into chunks.
- Slice nectarines in to thin crescent moon slivers (If they start to moosh, just go ahead and dice).
- With a Butcher knife, slice corn off cob into a mixing bowl.
- Add olives into bowl and mix lightly. No salt needed, the brine from the olives will do nicely.
- Add nectarines and mix lightly.

This is a delightful and refreshing twist. Pair with a unoaked Russian River **Sauvignon Blanc** or Carneros **Viognier**.

Sauvignon Blanc with its natural sharp herbal notes will feed off of the green olives and pimento, while the acidity will balance the creaminess of the corn jus and the briny element will contrast the sweetness of the nectarine.

Viognier will highlight the aromatics of the olives' fragrance and the fresh, "it's summer time!" smell of the nectarine and corn niblets.

Deliciouso!

Hip-Hop Jicama/Pear Slaw

Ingredients:
- 2 cups shredded Napa cabbage
- 1 (1 pound) jicama, peeled and shredded
- 2 cups shredded daikon radish
- 1 Granny Smith apple - peeled, cored and shredded
- 2 large carrots, shredded
- 2 firm Anjou or Bartlett pears, cored, quartered and thinly sliced
- 1/4 cup finely chopped cilantro
- 2 tablespoons extra virgin olive oil
- 3 tablespoons passion, mango, or orange juice (or tablespoon of each if feeling adventurous)
- 1 tablespoon lime juice
- 2 tablespoons toasted sesame seeds
- Sea salt and pepper to taste

Instructions:
» Place the cabbage, jicama, radish, apple, carrot, pear, and cilantro into a mixing bowl.
» Sprinkle with olive oil, orange juice, lime juice, salt, and pepper. Toss until evenly blended, sprinkle toasted seeds and serve. Simple as that!

Pair with an Anderson Valley **Gewurtztraminer** or **Riesling** as the tanginess of these wines and the natural acidity in the juices will bring to life the earthy flavors of the Jicama and cilantro as well as the mellow flavor of the pears.

Get jiggy widit!

Double Cut Brined Pork Chops

Ingredients:
4 Bone-in Double Cut Pork Chops (2 ribs protruding per cutlet)
- Sea Salt or Kosher Salt-enough to cover bottom of the Pyrex dish (about 2/3 cup)
- 1-12 ounce bottle/can Mango juice
- Fresh Ginger root-at least 2 inches long, roughly chopped
- 6-8 Fresh long sprigs Rosemary

Brine:
- In a medium size Pyrex dish (2' x 1') cover entire bottom with salt.
- Add Mango juice, fresh rosemary (separate needles from stem) and ginger.
- Lay chops on top and let steep for 4-8 hours, depending on your desire/temperament for salt. Flip chops over at whatever is your half way point.

To cook:
» Light a charcoal fire on the grill.
» Grill to desired wellness. I prefer medium-rare. (Keepin' it juiceh!)
» Try to make perfect grill lines, by turning chops at a 90 degree angle.
» Add additional fresh rosemary, ifya like.

Pork and **Pinot** *is always a classic match. You can always add the Grand Marnier infused Bing cherries to brighten the dish up.*

Because of the saltiness of the brine, a juicy (fruit forward) such as a Russian River or Santa Rita Hills **Pinot Noir** *is best.*

Bootylicious Braised Brussel Sprouts

Ingredients:
- 8-10 Brussel Sprouts (very green, no yellow leaves)
- ¼ cup Cashews, Slivered Almonds or Sunflower seeds
- 2-3 Mandarin Oranges or Tangerines
- ¼ cup sun-dried tomatoes, diced
- ¼ cup bacon fat grease (why you little piggy!), or equivalent of salted butter or Olive oil (or other vegetable oil) depending on your level of decadence or dietary restrictions.

Instructions:
» Peel mandarins and pull apart individual segments.
» Thoroughly wash vegetables, pad dry and cut off butt end if so desired cut in half from end-to-end. (Should look like a petite cabbage.)
» In a wok or high edge skillet, braise Brussels in bacon fat for 7-8 minutes on medium high heat, until they start to brown on cut side and outer leaves. Cook a little longer, if you don't like them al dente, but the fiber is better for you if you do.
» Add sundried tomatoes and toss.
» Remove from heat and place in serving bowls topping with orange segments and nuts. Voila!

Great to serve with the Double–cut Pork Chop. Excellent with a Monterey **Pinot Blanc**. The fruit in the wine will make a nice foil for the Mandarin Orange slices and tartness of the sun-drieds; the nuts will tie in the Oak barrel; the acidity of the wine will cut the fat of the bacon grease which will add character to the mellow Sprouts.

"Shake yo' Booty!"

Wonderful Waldorf Hysteria Salad
(Doin' the Twist on an all-time classic)

Ingredients:
- 4 Granny Smith apples (about 4 cups)
- Or, one each of your favs, maybe Pink Lady, Golden Delicious, Pippin, Red Delicious
- 2/3 cup salted whole Cashew nuts or Marcona Almonds
- ½ cup Golden Raisins
- 4 celery ribs
- ½ Jicama (about 6 ounces)
- 1 Eureka lemon
- ½ cup Avocado Mayonnaise or Marie's Blue Cheese dressing
- 1/3 cup Maytag or Point Reyes Bleu Cheese (optional)

Instructions:
- Peel off skin of a half of Jicama, cut into strips and then into ¼ inch pieces.
- Place Jicama in a small bowl, and squeeze the Eureka juice over top. Let marinate for 30 minutes, mixing from time to time to coat.
- In the meantime, wash, core and cut apples into ¾ inch pieces, leaving skin on.
- Chop celery ribs into ¼ inch pieces.
- Transfer apples and celery into a large mixing bowl and scoop in the mayo or dressing, coating thoroughly. Refrigerate until Jicama is ready and then add to mixture, tossing thoroughly.
- Spoon out apples, celery and jicama into salad bowls.
- Top each off with (in this order) Goldens, then nuts, and finish with Bleu crumbles.

If using all Granny Smith Apples, pair with a stainless steel fermented **Sauvignon Blanc** from Mendocino or Lake Counties, as the high level of both the wine and the Grannys will counter balance. If using other types of apples not as crisp (acidic), then try an **Albarino** from Lodi or a partial barrel fermented Sonoma Valley **Sauvignon Blanc**.

8

California Wine Marketing

In the mid to late 1980's, I worked for a small, but extremely impressive portfolio of California Wineries. Tom Heller was the owner, and he had quite a knack for seeking out and discovering super high quality boutique wineries in Napa and Sonoma that were just getting started and needed a marketing arm to get in the door and get distribution in the finest restaurants and high end wine retailers throughout the state of California. Tom hired me as the Regional Manager for San Diego.

Heller's company, California Wine Marketing's stable was: Caymus, Shafer, Iron Horse, Forman, Altimura, The Hess Collection, Matanzas Creek, Keenan, Swanson, Alexander Valley Vineyards, Merry (Edwards) Vintners, B.R. Cohn, Dehlinger, Mazzocco, Sinskey, Signorello, St. Clement and Arrowood. An impressive lot, especially in those early days of the Golden Age of California Wine.

One of my bigger on –premise accounts as a Broker in San Diego was the Summer House Inn in La Jolla., home of "Elario's" Restaurant, where I would become the first ever non-winemaker, to host a "Dinner with the Winemaker".

Several stories up on the top floor was Elarios with a spectacular view of the Pacific Ocean overlooking La Jolla cove. I thought this to be the ideal place to really establish myself, entrench me as a serious player in this marketplace and spotlight these soon to be very prestigious Brands. I put together by invitation only exclusive tasting for my top tier accounts. As an additional part of the draw, we had a guest celebrity, NFL Hall of Famer, Dan Fouts. Dan is one of *the* nicest men you could ever meet! *SO*, down to earth. He led the "Air Coryell" offensive attack as the starting Quaterback for the San Diego Chargers for 14 years. The room was even more electric when he entered the room, and with an already impressive and influential group of guests from this elite wine-centric community.

Fortunately for Dan, he had just left the event and missed the final person to enter the room as were all breaking down our respective stations and were out of wine. Much to the disappointment of this uninvited final entrant. As he started to loosen his tie, still with his sport jacket on, he quickly and furiously surveyed the room to no avail-nobody had any wine on any of the dozen tables! That wasn't stopping him! He glared around the room like he was set up for some kind of conspiracy and immediately proceeded to grab the extremely full dump bucket and proceeded to down it-this was *LONG (20+ years)* before Miles' character in Sideways copied this vile action.

John Skupny of Caymus, Peter Rubens of Keenan and myself lunged toward the man, screaming "NOOOOOOOooooooooooo...."

But alas, it was too late...I didn't think it was very attractive sport jacket anyway.

Martin, the owner of the Summer House Inn, was a big fan of the Mayacamas Winery. He had collected a huge amount of their Cabernet Sauvignon, and the vertical was growing ever larger. He contacted Bob Travers, the original owner and winemaker to come down to host a winemaker dinner at Elarios. Bob never returned any of Martin's calls. (This was pre e-mail days.) The collection was expanding. For some reason, dinner guests visiting San Diego were not ordering a lot of intense mountain cabernet with their fish-oh yeah! The old, archaic rule of red wine with meat, white wine with fish was still *sanctimonious.*

So, Martin, ever the introvert, turned to me and asked if I would be interested in being Master of Ceremonies for his Mayacamas wine dinner.

"Would I? Oh HELLYEAH!"

Little did I know then that this would become the precursor to me hosting and conducting hundreds of dinners and events that would ultimately become *the show and the character 'Sandrew, the Napa and Sonoma Wine Sherpa'.*

It was 1987. The commercial internet wouldn't be launched until 1993. I was desperate to get information on Travers and Mayacamas-any marketing collateral-anything at all. He wouldn't return my calls either and there was no web to research, no Googling. Finally I left a message on Bob's phone machine-'member those?

"Bob. Sandrew Montgomery here. Hey I'm doin' a Mayacamas Winemaker Dinner at Elarios in La Jolla. You should be doing this, but I'm happy to do it. I just need some background info-any marketing materials you have would be greatly appreciated, so that I can do a stellar job for you."

Nothing. Nada. Never heard a word.

Ok. Guess I'm on my own. I know I can wing it-but I really want to deliver. I wanted to WOW the audience. After all, these folks are spending $75 per person in 1987 dollars, for god's sake!

As that evening got started-I didn't realize this at the time-but, as I got centered to go on, "Sandrew the Napa and Sonoma Wine Sherpa" was born. And as the evening continued, I was in the zone: the vibe felt right, the buzz in the dining room was intoxicating along with the convivial conversations and laughter in between wine presentations. 'I'm really pulling this off! ', I thought to myself. We were just about ready for the dessert course.

<u>And then it hit me!</u>

How am I going to wrap this up? I had not thought that through. Oh Shit!

So I got up from my table, one last time, walked around the room from table to table, asking all the patrons how the evening was for them-everyone was so encouraging as people are prone to be when they have a belly full of great wine and inspiring cuisine. I found myself at one end of the room and moving towards the middle. I started spouting out all the descriptors and adjectives of the night, spotlighting the more esoteric ones and concluded with: "But you know what folks? It's just grape juice and either you like or you don't. That's all that matters."

With my hand extended high, I waved to the crowd and exclaimed "Thanks for coming!"

And with that, the entire room stood up and applauded. I believe I sorta bowed and then just kept on walking…there was nothing else to say…I found myself in the kitchen. I looked at Chef and thanked him, shook hands, and took the kitchen elevator to the lobby and that was it. This was pre "fist pumping". But that was the feeling I had walking to my car. I got into my little car, turned the engine on and heard myself: *Well, that was cool!*

In the early "70's, one of my favorite bands was the Doobie Brothers. Man I loved to hear Tommy Johnston's voice on China Grove, Listen to the Music and Long Train Comin'. And Pat Simmons-what a great ol' Soul-you can see it in his eyes, especially in person, as I did backstage when I met him, Tommy and Michael McDonald. The Doobie Brothers Manager, Bruce Cohn bought a special property called Olive Hill between Sonoma Mountain and the Mayacamas, in the little village of Glen Ellen in Sonoma County. The Doobies had broken up and Bruce decide it was time for his new career as "wine maker"-or at least Proprietor of a winery, and thus B.R.Cohn Winery was birthed. Unfortunately the original wine maker for the 1984 and 1985 Olive Hill Cabernet Sauvignon had passed away before the release of these two stellar wines. Bruce was left with no choice but to turn to his cellar rat: "You worked closest with John. Now you'll have to take over."

And that's how Rock Star Winemaker Helen Turley got her start!

Of course the Doobie Brothers did get back together (as the have many times) and toured, leaving Bruce to turn to us at California Wine Marketing to broker his wine, that Robert Parker absolutely adored. I have to say the 2 of them were mind blowing reds and two of my all-time epiphany wines.

I had seen the Doobies at Red Rocks Amphitheater in Colorado, but Bruce got me backstage and introduced me to them in San Diego.

One of my client's, Ernst of his namesake restaurant "Ernie's", was the former Executive Chef for Jimmy Carter when he was President. Now Ernst's girth was- well let's just say he *looked like a chef!* He was from Austria and had a *very* thick accent as well. When we launched (introduced) B.R. Cohn I asked Ernst if he had ever heard of B.R. Cohn:

"B, AH Cone… B, AH Cone-oh yah! Da DOO bee Bruddahs!"

"Oh you *do* know who they are-guess I should send you 3 cases!" I said winking, and he did put the Olive Hill Cabernet on his wine list and took the 3 cases.

Now Bruce created the annual Sonoma Fall Music festival always with the Doobs headlining, a benefit to raise money for several Sonoma charities. It even had celebrity golf tournament followed by a gourmet dinner and auctions throughout the weekend.

Huey Lewis, Bruce Cohn, Tommy Smothers with fellow golfers

One year after the devastating hurricane, Katrina walloped New Orleans, the concert benefitted those victims. There is even a DVD filmed on October 2, 2005, of the concert and the first person you see dancin' is my wife Kat in the lime green top. She even got up on stage and sang "So Happy Together" with Flo' and Eddie of the Turtles!

When I proposed to Kat on Valentine's Day, 1998, it was at the Lark Creek in Larkspur. Huey Lewis happened to be there too and this was the second time I met him at this fabulous Marin County establishment. Feeling like old friends now, Huey came up to me at the bar and said: "You just come in here and order anything you want?!" "Hey man, howya doin' Huey?" I was going to offer to buy him a drink, but his breath and his comment revealed that maybe this should be his last scotch of the evening. Anyway, I informed the Bartender that I would be proposing. That night, owner/celebrity Chef Bradley Ogden himself delivered a chocolate cake to our table with "Congratulations!" written in chocolate around the perimeter of the plate. What a nice touch.

I sold a ton of wine to the Hotel del Coronado, the Grande Dame Hotel featured prominently in the movie "Some Like it Hot" with Marilyn Monroe and Tony Curtis. Thanks to Joy Sterling for making the original placements, as the Hotel del was my largest Iron Horse account. The buyer there loved the "Wedding Cuvee" and poured it by the glass, as so many honeymooners would frequent this beautiful establishment on the shores of Coronado Island where I would become the opening Wine Director and Sommelier for Peohe's Restaurant. Iron Horse's Winemaker, Forrest Tancer who, along with Joy's parents, Audrey and Barry Sterling, started this California Sparkling house in Sonoma's Russian River/Green Valley in 1976. Forrest watched Joy grow up and unbeknownst to her, was in love with her. When Joy announced to Forrest that she was engaged to be married, a very disappointed Tancer reluctantly but graciously congratulated her. For Joy's wedding day, Forrest crafted the first ever "Wedding Cuvee" in her honor as his gift to the couple. As it turns out, that marriage did not work out and Joy was now available. Forrest did not hesitate to express that he had been in love with her all this time. They started dating and ended up getting married themselves!

Some of my other San Diego clients were the top Restaurateurs of the day: Kip Downing of the three Pacifica restaurants, Stephen Zolezzi of Stephano's and Bertrand Hug of Mille Fleurs. I had the opportunity to fly them to Mazzocco Winery and Vineyards in Healdsburg, courtesy of Tom Mazzocco and his private Cessna. The airport is literally next door; very convenient as we were only there for the day. And what a day it was!

It was a Fall classic, beautiful day in California, as we flew over a big chunk of the State. Once we landed, it took us a minute and half to get to the understated Dry Creek Valley winery where we were sipping on Chardonnay and given a tour by the winemaker, Nancy. She thiefed out of barrel several samples of Cab and Zinfandel. Then it was on to a simple but deliciously prepared lunch on the patio overlooking the vineyards. Gorgeous. I told 'the boys' about Tom and his ingenious innovations including the collapsible golf clubs. Well of course, having had a fair amount of wine, the fellas all being golfers, said they had to check this out themselves. Out came the clubs and golf balls and the goofballs had a blast, smacking those little white dimply things into the vineyards across the way!

Bertrand, the ridiculously handsome Frenchman, who was wearing a stunning royal blue French cuffed shirt had managed to spill an *entire glass* of Cabernet on himself and his shirt in the heat of the excitement of driving those Titleists into the Zinfandel plantings.

We all had a good laugh at his expense (Wine Away did not exist then). He laughed too. It was time to head back to the airport and back to "America's Finest City". Monsieur Hug asked me if I would drive him to his restaurant in very affluent Rancho Santa Fe as he had a very important dinner to attend to. Of course I accepted and asked him on the drive up on Highway 5 who was the dinner for?

"Lloyd Bentsen. It's a fundraiser. Thousand bucks a head." Bentsen was running for Vice President on Michael Dukakis' Democratic ticket in 1988. Just a few weeks before, Lloyd had famously shot down Dan Quayle (Mr. Potatoe head) regarding his qualifications and experience in the October 5th debate:

Quayle: "*I have as much experience as Jack Kennedy had when he sought the Presidency.*"

Bentsen: "Senator, I served with Jack Kennedy. I knew Jack Kennedy. Jack Kennedy was a friend of mine. Senator, you're no Jack Kennedy."

As I was dropping Bertrand off at the front of his restaurant- red wine stained royal blue shirt and all-he jumped out of my car and started racing to the door, promptly greeted by 2 Secret Servicemen who stopped him immediately in his tracks, forcing all 4 stiff arms into his chest.

"Where do you think you're going?" one of them interrogated gruffly.

"This is my restaurant-I'm late and I gotta get in there!"

"Sure you do buddy." Looking him up and down and fixating on the red wine stained shirt.

"No really. I'm the owner-just ask anyone inside!"

I tried yelling through the passenger side, as in his haste, Bertrand left the car door wide open. "He *IS* the owner!" I exclaimed. Of course they thought I was the getaway driver and in cahoots.

Finally the door opened from inside and Mr. Hug was properly identified and allowed in.

On one of my 'workwiths', as we call them on the wholesale side of the business, where you are working with one of your suppliers, Doug Shafer of Shafer Vineyards in Stags Leap was riding along with me. I consider his Dad, John, who I also worked with, a mentor because of his entrepreneurial spirit, having left a substantial publishing career in Chicago to risk everything and start his own winery. He was also a big proponent of getting the Stags Leap district to become an official AVA (American Viticultural Area) and succeeded in 1989. This of course is also home to Stag's Leap Wine Cellars SLV made by Warren Winiarski which took first place in the Paris Tasting of 1976. The Cabernets made here are said to be "the iron fist in the velvet glove".

It was late in the afternoon, that Doug and I went to one of my restaurant accounts on Point Loma. As we entered the seafood house, I told him "I'll go get the buyer and you can just hang right here." I walked down the corridor to the office and could see she was on the phone in her office. I looked over at the pay phone booth in the hallway ('member pay phones?) and thought I better check in with my wife (first wife, Lorry). After I hung up with her, I walked back to Doug in the main part of the restaurant with a white, glazed face and a blank stare.

"What's the matter? The Buyer not going to meet with us?"

"No…no…"

"Well what is it?"

"Uh…um…I just found out my wife is… uh"

"She ok?" Doug quickly asked.

"…pregnant. She's pregnant." I mumbled.

Doug immediately bear hugged me, lifted me off the ground and started bouncing us up and down and out into the parking lot, exclaiming, "That's great! We're having a baby, we're having a babeee!"

And that's how I learned about Robert Starling Montgomery IV coming into the world! *Woo-HOOOOooooooo!*

In the fall of 2001, I went to visit Caymus Vineyards in Rutherford of the famed "Rutherford Dust", as Andre' Tchelistcheff coined it. I always loved (and still do) their Cabernets and Zinfandels and had the good fortune to sell them in their early days and even to launch "Conundrum". I worked both with Charlie Wagner and his son Chuck, the founders of Caymus. One of my first 'epiphany wines' was the Caymus 1982 Pinot Noir-it seduced me! In 1989, the influential Wine Spectator magazine named Caymus' 1984 Special Selection Cabernet its wine of the year, and in 1994 it awarded that honor to the 1990 Special Selection. The only wine to ever repeat, and this is with over 17,000 wines from around the world rated/tasted annually! I had just started with California Wine Marketing when Wine Spectator's new issue that had this cover on the front:

Two years later, I sold **500 cases** of Caymus Napa Cabernet to <u>one</u> account!

Being a hundred percent commission guy, I had to go home that day and change my underwear!!

I first met Charlie and Chuck at Tra Vigne for a CWM dinner, which had just opened and featured a young unknown Chef named Michael Chiarello. At that dinner, we drank alotta wine, including several of that fabulous 1984 Special Selection Cabernet.

Charlie was very soft spoken and deliberate man, a farmer first and winemaker second. When that "Best Damn Cabernet" Wine Spectator, came out, it was a very audacious statement, but no one ever questioned it. Charlie's humble response? "I don't know what all the fuss is about. It's just grape juice. I'm glad they like it." Maybe *that's* where I got that from.

One day Kat and I were down in downtown Santa Barbara checking out "the Wine Ghetto", a re-gentrified community of old warehouse and garages now converted to Wine Tasting rooms for several excellent local small producers. As I was talking to some fellow tourists, somehow we got on Caymus and I mentioned that I worked with Charlie Wagner. This young man in his early twenties came up to me and said. "I went to high school with Charlie!" I looked at him quizzically and a bit irritated, smacked him on the elbow, and responded, "I'm talking about his grandfather thank you very much!"

There's a story about Charlie (Senior!) and his buddy, Mr. Kelham who would help out in the makeshift tasting room in the early days. As legend has it, they would start at 10:00 in the morning opening up the wines and tasting them from the bottom of the menu upwards. The bottom of the menu was "port". As the day wore on and the 'testing' of the wines continued, by closing time at 4:00 o'clock, they would be in the back, cleaning up. If there was knock on the door, they would yell out rather boisterously "you better be buyin' or were not commin' out!"

So on that Fall day in 2001, as I strolled out of the parking lot on the way to the updated version of the tasting room, there was Charlie tending to his garden in the front of the winery.

"Hello Charlie! Great to see you out here gardening. I don't know if you remember me, but I sold your wines for many years in San Diego through California Wine Marketing and again in San Francisco with JALCo." I extended my hand, "Sandrew Montgomery".

"Oh yes, Sandrew. Nice to see *you* again." Charlie said as we shook hands.

"Those were different times then", he continued. Things are very different today. The Valley has changed *so* much. When I first got here, there was mostly walnut orchards and plum trees and cattle ranches. Now it's almost all grapes and wineries. And they just keep building more wineries-it's hard to keep up."

As we talked more about those changes and the good ol' days, feeling the late summer California sun burning down on us, I made mention of Joe Heitz recent passing. "Yeah he was quite a character." Charlie said with an old world wink.

"I used to sell his wine too," I said. "He was a bit of a cantankerous man. His marketing strategy was: 'Well what are those bastards down the street getting for their wine? Well let's raise ours $5 a bottle more. Ours is better than theirs!' He also did not like people referring to his Martha's Vineyard Cab as minty or Eucalyptus. "Eucalyptus smells like cat piss and there ain't no goddamn cat pee in my wine!' Yep! Pretty cantankerous guy-but a helluva winemaker," I added.

As Mr. Wagner and I were talking, I thought to myself, wow man, I have all these stories about the pioneers of the golden age of the California wine industry, and *somebody* needs to tell them. Four or five months later, Charlie passed away. Not long after that, Justin Meyer of Silver Oak passed. Yeah, somebody needs to preserve their memories and tell these stories all right.

9

Back to San Francisco

I had made a promise to myself that I would come back to San Francisco within 10 years from my departure in 1982-and *this time* I would be ready. And I made good on that promise, but my brilliant move was on June 21st, 1992-on the first day of Summer from San Diego! We arrived in the Sunset district at 11:30 at night. The fog was in-it was FREEEEEEZING! What the hell was I thinking?! I immediately got all of our winter coats from Colorado, which of course were conveniently all the way in the back of the 28 foot U-Haul.

I was hired to be the San Francisco Wine Supervisor managing a small team of sales people for JALCo, a Seagrams' House owned by the Bronfmans. The President of JALCo was Lou Palatella, a hulking man as he played Offensive Guard for the San Francisco Forty-Niners. As intimidating as his presence was, he was heckuva nice guy. Often he would have his side kick, 49er Tackle Hall of Famer Bob St. Claire with him for lunch. For Bob, always a steak-raw-not rare-raw! I think Lou did this just to blow our minds in the company cafeteria. Our National Accounts rep was Janet Dyer who invited me to Bon Appetite's tasting panel with Anthony Dias Blue. The embargo had just been lifted from South Africa after ten years, and we were the first to taste wines from this area of the world with Pinotages.

One of my big accounts was the famed Fairmont Hotel on Nob Hill. This has been the palace to many a glamorous movie star, foreign diplomat, politicians' choice of residency, as well as to many of the highest net worth individuals from around the globe. On one particular night, I brought then wife Lorry to dinner. When I entered into the dining room, I did my best Warren Beatty and acted is if I was a foreign dignitary, perusing the room, dipping below one eye. I immediately recognized a gentleman sitting at his table awaiting guests.

He gave me that 'I know you' look and smiled big with a twinkle in his eyes squinted just underneath his bushy eyebrows. I approached Ernest and extended my hand. "How are you, Mr. Gallo? Nice to see you this evening!"

He continued that all knowing smile and winked, "Nice to see *you*!" was his reply. I thought I had better get to *my* table before I was found out!

Another time at the Fairmont, I had a great private meeting with Jean Charles Boisset, also known as JCB(who, ironically is married to Gina Gallo). I had worked with him (but mostly his father, Jean Claude Boisset) in Denver at Western Davis Distributing and now again with the two men from Burgundy at JALCo. JCB and I have met on several occasions and chide each other about stealing each others' ideas. He is a creative genius, 24/7!

Another one of my SF accounts was a brand new retail wine shop on Filmore Street, called PlumpJack. It was just one guy, the founder running the place, Gavin Newsom. Nice guy, this Gavin Newsom. But I couldn't figure out why his end stacks had knights in shining armor and this funky mirror that looked like he got it from an old Horror House and fake shields on the walls with fake hand drawn swords. I mean, I knew he was new to this business and he seemed like a bright young guy-but talk about old school. Maybe Gavin's just eccentric-after all his cousin was his partner and investor, Gordon Getty, yes, *that Gordon Getty*.

I sold Gavin a shit ton of wine for him to resell in his first location.

Gavin grew the PlumpJack group into a very expansive and successful company which includes PlumpJack, CADE and Odette wines and wineries, all in Napa.

- **1992** – PlumpJack Wine & Spirits, Marina location
- **1995** – PlumpJack Squaw Valley Inn
- **1995** – PlumpJack Cafe, Squaw Valley
- **1995** – PlumpJack Balboa Cafe, San Francisco
- **1997** – PlumpJack Estate Winery
- **2001** – PlumpJack Wine & Spirits, Noe Valley location
- **2001** – MatrixFillmore
- **2002** – PlumpJackSport, Squaw Valley
- **2003** – The Carneros Inn*
- **2004** – The Boon Fly Café*
- **2006** – FARM at The Carneros Inn*
- **2007** – PlumpJackSport at The Carneros Inn*
- **2007** – The Orchard Residences*
- **2007** – CADE Estate Winery
- **2008** – Balboa Cafe Mill Valley

2012 – Odette Estate Winery
2015 – Forgery
2015 – VERSO
2015 – Winery on Howell Mountain (Name TBD)
2016 – Hideaway Carmel
2016 – Wildhawk Bar
2016 – Melvyn's Restaurant, Palm Springs
2016 – Ingleside Inn, Palm Springs

Gavin Newsome was Mayor when I lived in the City. When Kat and I moved to Larkspur, we rented a house 2 doors down from where Newsom grew up. From time to time, I would play hoops on the same basketball court Gavin grew up playing on. As of this writing, he is Lieutenant Governor and running for Governor. Let's see where his political career takes him…

10

Grateful

Mickey, Woody, Bobby, Bonnie, Bruce, Phil and Santana

I have joked for decades that I have been trying to get away from the Grateful Dead since 1975 and it's still not working. It's *still* not working. Just ask my wife.

Often people will ask me, what brought me to California.

"It's the wine-theGratefulDeah-uh, the wine. It's the *wine*."

"Did you say the Grateful Dead?"

"Yeah, well, ok-it was **both**!"

My high school buddies introduced me to the music then with 2 albums: "American Beauty" and "Skull and Roses" albums (yes on vinyl!). I was surprised how much I liked the music-didn't know *anything* about them and was trying to be open minded but that…that name.

When I went to DU, I thought I was through with them. *Ha!*

My freshman year, I met quite a few Californians and they were all into the Dead. The first Dead show I went to wasn't until 1980 which was the 15th anniversary of the band, playing at Folsom field in Boulder, Colorado. Of course I went to both Saturday and Sunday shows dancin' my ass off, 'cause that's what you do. All my college buddies were there, Californian's, East Coasters and one guy from Denver named Tom Poole.

Tom grew up in Denver's Cherry Hills and went to school with a kid named Tim Duncan whose father started Silver Oak with partner and winemaker Justin Meyer. Tom and his wife Lauri (a very dear friend of mine) who also went to the University of Denver with us, had 3 sons and lived in Mill Valley, right next door to Bob Weir, singer and guitarist of the Grateful Dead! Bobby is also quite a fan of wine and Burgundies in particular. I know this because he and I have had multiple discussions bandying about the merits and differences of red Burgundy and California and Oregonian Pinots, terroir, negotiants and other topics related to wine.

The first two times I met Weir were at the Hunan Restaurant in San Francisco, where we met at the bar discussing and arguing the virtues of our mutually favorite red grape. The Hunan is a great place to go after a Dead show to eat those red devil peppers in the Kung Pao shrimp to rid all those toxins incurred and ingested by being at these legendary concerts.

Tom introduced me to the Tamalpais Chiefs, a Marin County flag football team that Bobby Weir quarterbacked. One afternoon before a show at the Shoreline Amphitheater, we had just enough time to play a pickup game. I have a few bootleg tapes where Bob and Jerry Garcia are asking the audience to step back to make some room for the Deadheads in front, as "they are all getting real bug-eyed."

One show in particular Weir says, "Take a step back. And yet another *step back* and yet, another *step baaaaack*!" So on one of the plays, Bobby directs me as a wide receiver: "Sandrew go down field to the left and take a step back and then another step back", as he is drawing this out in the palm of his hand. "Are you fuckin' kidding me?!" I'm saying to myself as I'm hearing this casette that I have heard reeling over and over in my head for three decades.

This was in the early 1990's and the band had lost yet another of their keyboard players, Brent Mydland, and now Bruce Hornsby was part of the Grateful Dead. We were in Bobby's dressing room after our little flag football game and Hornsby was there too. "Thanks for joining the band, Bruce" I said to him. "I don't know how else to say this, but your piano has really 'prettied up' the sound. It's been getting kinda edgy lately, and I think you have been instrumental in taking the edge off-no pun intended!" "None taken!" He replied and smiled. "And thank you for saying that."

Tom Poole was playing softball in Marin one evening in 1995 and at age 33, just keeled over in the outfield. He had suddenly died of a brain aneurysm. At 33! Holy Shit!

When we celebrated Tom's life at the Poole's house in Mill Valley, Bobby Weir was there with Woody Harrelson. We toasted Tom, laughed about him playing hacky sack in shorts with black cowboy boots and smoked a few joints. It was a shocking and sad occasion, but Tom would have wanted us to carry on that way.

The next time I saw Woody Harrelson was in Sausilito. I almost ran him over as I was parking the car. Kat and I were going to lunch at Cavello Point. I dropped her off at the base of the long set of cement stairs and immediately found a parking spot in the front. As I started parallel parking, I noticed this motorcycle dude in black leather attire with a cherry red helmet in my rearview mirror, zipping in right behind me. WHOOOOA!

I got outta my car and started to apologize. "Dude! Almost hit you-sorry 'bout tha…" and he took his helmet off.

"Woody?!" Sure'nuff it was the comedian from "Cheers!" turned actor and activist.

"Hey man. Sandrew Montgomery" I said as I extended my hand out. "You and I met in Mill Valley at Tom Poole's wake with Weir."

"Ohyeah." Harrelson said, somewhat recalling.

"I just saw you on the news climbing the Golden Gate Bridge protesting." I mentioned as I was pointing to the Golden Gate Bridge literally directly behind him.

"Oh yeah. That. Had to do it!"

"Well good to see you, man. My wife's in there waiting for me for lunch." I told Woody as I headed up the stairs. Kat and I had I good laugh as I told her what had just occurred.

I met Grateful Dead drummer Mickey Hart (and my best friend Steve Hart's cousin) at the San Rafael Fairgrounds just before a show his band's "Planet Drum" was about to play. It was his father who was the original Grateful Dead's manager who ripped them off, which inspired the song "He's Gone" and the lyrics "steal your face right off your head". This in turn inspired the iconic Steal Your Face symbol also adorned on one time keyboardist Keith Godchaux's Grand Piano, an album cover and countless tie-dyed T-shirts:

Kat and I re-enacted our wedding and had the reception at our good friends the Dergosits home in San Rafael. I choreographed <u>9 hours</u> of music. First set was with the smooth jazz, moving into Island Music, the Beach Boys, and all things Reggae while we were enjoying the Hawaiin Luau. Second set, was Soul, Mowtown and Funk-let the dancing begin! And then for set three-we were ROCKIN'! We had the Stones and JGeils and of course, many of my friends being Deadheads, well…I had envisioned how this would end in my head. Sho' nuff, right when the Grateful Dead were playing Chuck Berry's "Around and Around" and singing: "They nevah stopped rockin' till the PO-lice knocked", there were the cops at the end of the driveway doing that "cut" motion with their hands across the throat.

When Kat and I lived in Marin, invariably we would run in to Phil and Jill, of course Phil Lesh, the bass player for the Grateful Dead. We'd run in to them and sometimes their two sons with our two sons, Robby and Clifton, whether it was breakfast, lunch or dinner. When the horrendous apocalyptic wildfires of 2017 devastated Napa and even more so Sonoma (our former home in Glen Ellen of 9 years was completely demolished along with all of our old neighbors) we evacuated back to Marin. The last room available left in the Bay Area was a little hole in the wall motel right underneath the intersection of the incredibly noisy 24/7 overpass of freeways 101 and 880. Believe me, we were *GRATEFUL!*

Phil's Terrapin Crossroads restaurant was just a mile and half away so on that Tuesday night, October 10th, we had dinner with Phil. Rather appropriate, I suppose.

More Rockstars

The first time I saw Carlos Santana on stage was in Jacksonville, Florida. He was opening for Eric Clapton-whatta incredible double bill! I think I was just 14 or 15. Santana was one of my favorite acts in the original Woodstock movie. Of course it was raining like hell, and when the Grateful Dead got on stage, they kept getting shocked and electrocuted by their musical equipment. (Now of course they were the house band for the Electric Koolaid Acid tests, but this was not part of the show!) From that point forward, they would always have carpets on stage. They started that trend (too) and every musical act to this day has carpets on stage just so they won't get shocked.

The next time I saw Santana was in Denver at McNichols Arena where the Feyline Productions' security wore shiny yellow jackets. They were harassing some poor bastard dancing in the aisles (no it wasn't me). In mid-song, Carlos turns to the band, waves his hand in the air to 'cut', walks to the mic and says" You! In the yellow jackets-*cool out* man!" Now "chill out" was a saying of the day, as was "coolit". But "cool out"? That was Carlos, spiritual guy that he is, was like a demigod and security immediately stopped upon command and the Santana Band commenced right where they left off mid-song. How cool is that?!

Of course, Santana being an 'instrumental' part of the San Fransisco Sound and scene would often play with the Grateful Dead for Bill Graham or the Family Dog.

When Kat and I lived in Marin, we often frequented Il Fornio restaurant in Corte Madera. It was one of my very good wine accounts as a distributor and right next door to Larkspur. Carlos and his wife also like to frequent the Il Fornio. One afternoon we spotted them lunching just behind the fireplace. I sent over a couple of glasses of wine over to their table. As Carlos looked up from the table and around to see who had sent wine his way, I raised my glass toward him and said, "Thanks for all the great concerts. Cheers!"

"Salud. Gracious!" was all he said back; that's all he needed to say.

In my somewhat brief high tech days, I attended the E-3 Trade convention in Los Angeles. It was one of the loudest damn things I've ever attended, second only to a Robert Plant concert where I lost my hearing for 3 days-but hey! I was dancin'!

E-3 was so loud and obnoxious I wanted to get out of there, but since I flew down from the Bay area just for this, I needed to do some business development. Which ended up being mostly just picking up business cards where I would later follow up with a phone call to next generation software and multi-media startups that I wanted to do business with. As I was moving swiftly through the various vendor booths picking up business cards, I stumbled upon on one presenters' vacant booth with a small placard. It read: "Join us tonight for a free concert with Carlos Santana for our launch tonight". WTF?! Really? This can't be. I visited a few other booths nearby, but kept eyeing back, until finally somebody showed up. "Is this for real?" I asked as I pointed to the placard.

"Yup. Tonight at the Palladium."

"For free? For real?" I kept saying in disbelief.

"Yes. For real. See, here are 2 tickets for you." She smiled and handed me the tickets.

My response? "Fuckin' A!" ...Oh! And **Thank** you. Thank you *very* much!"

I was staying in Hollywood with my sister, Beth, and immediately called her.

"Beth! We're going to see Carlos Santana tonight! I just got 2 free tickets! Woo-Hoo!"

"Whaaaaat?"

"Yeah really. I'm coming back to your house right now and leaving this trade show."

On my way out, I was feeling pretty guilty about cutting this trip so short, so I thought I'd stop at just one more booth to justify leaving so early. So I spotted this one called "PayPal". I talked to this one young guy, very entrepreneurial, who was genuinely excited about his service. In his calm yet enthusiastic South

African accent he said to me "This will be the wave of the future. It will change how we conduct business on the internet."

"Of course it will", I smiled somewhat insincerely and dismissingly. I thought to myself, "He has to say that. Just another guy trying to make a buck in the internet space-what does he know." As I walked out the door I briefly glanced at his card; some guy named Elon Musk.

So Beth and I arrive at the Palladium and there are all these exotic, beautiful brightly colored costumed dancers parading around us like peacocks. Fantastic!

I immediately b-lined it to the front of the stage, dead center. Beth and I stood there for forty-five minutes to an hour, then the house lights dropped and the band comes out and strikes up the chords to "Smooth" which was just about to be released with the whole sensational "Supernatural" album/CD/record that brought Santana back into the mainstream and introduced his talents to a whole new generation.

The concert was flawless, colorful and spectacular! Towards the end, some of the ol' Santana classics came out like "Black Magic Woman" and "Oye Coma Va" and one that transcended me back to the day, I believe it was "Everything's Commin' Our Way" or maybe it was "Song of the Wind" which transformed me into the San Francisco psychedelic cosmic space noodle. It just soothed my soul spiritually and made my heart soar.

There was a brief break before the next song. Carlos was like thirteen feet in front of us, so I said in a rather calm, above a whisper but somewhat quiet voice, "Thank you, Carlos." With that, he bowed in Namaste fashion with his hands clasped together in appreciation, moving a step back. The band immediately proceeded into "Maria Maria". (The only song I did not dance to that night.)

What a delightful evening!

A week later "Supernatural" came out and once again Santana songs filled the radio air waves. It went straight to number one on the charts.

Several years after that, Kat and I were in Mill Valley walking on the sidewalk heading toward town. This lady was driving *very* slowly, parallel to us headed in the same direction. Behind her was a generic looking white van. The driver, growing impatient with her, proceeded to drive up over the curb on to the edge of the sidewalk. The window was rolled down on the passengers' side was a guy in black beanie cap looking back to make sure his buddy didn't hit us.

"Carlos"?! He looked back at us, waived and smiled. His buddy just kept on driving-though back on the street!

When I was kid living in Georgia and going to high school, I had the opportunity to guest DJ on a local radio station. I got to introduce a new album by Bonnie Raitt and her cover of Lil' Runaway. I had not heard of Bonnie Raitt (yet) and since we had no rehearsal, when I read the script live on the air, my pronunciation came out Bonnie <u>Rat.</u> I was later informed (off air, thankgod) how to properly pronounce her last name. (It was probably to all of 3 listeners anyway, but I still felt bad about it.)

The first time I met Bonnie was at a Fundraiser in San Francisco where I was pouring wine and she was the evenings' Entertainer. I had to pee before I got stuck behind my table and as I was going down the stairs, Bonnie was coming up the stairs. Because she looked so 'familiar' (how could I not recognize her with her trademark white streak down the middle of her beautiful red hair?)

I started to ask her do you know where the bathroom is? Instead, what came out was, "Do you know where the bathroo-oh I can't ask you that." Her response: "What? You don't think you can ask me where the bathroom is?"

"Well, no maam. I mean, yes, well, I guess I *could*."

"It's ok. Down the stairs, down the hall to the right." "Thank you!" And I ran down the stairs in nervous embarrassment. As I stood there in front of the urinal peeing, I thought to myself, "Damn! I should have apologized to her about mispronouncing her name two and a half decades earlier." She sounded awesome that night-I even caught myself dancing behind the table to a few of her tunes. I have seen her in concert another 3 or 4 times since that fateful run in, most recently at Pacbell Park with James Taylor.

Ms. Raitt also played with Bobby. Phil, Mickey and Billy after Jerry Garcia died. The show was at the legendary Warfield-it was killer and classic! My friend, Elissa Anderman produced this private and intimate dinner and concert, so I got to meet and greet Bonnie after the show and was *not* going to miss this opportunity to correct this, this time.

I told her about the radio show and introduce her new hit-" I said 'and this is Bonnie Rat's new song'-I'm *so* sorry I didn't know how to pronounce your name and it just came out wrong-I'm a huge fan of yours and would never intentionally call you a rat." "That's ok," she calmly laughed and politely responded in her soft Southern drawl, "I never knew."

11

Crazy Horse (The Neil Young story)

In High School, I took a poetry class and our assignment was to pick a poet and write an essay about them. It was the seventies, so while classmates picked traditional poets like e.e. cummings and Robert Frost, I thought it would be cool to think differently and so chose Neil Young. Crosby, Stills, Nash and Young had a big influence on my musical tastes and opinions-the lyrics *were* important and appealed to my inner Hippie-so why not be unconventional? Now remember, I had seen the Beatles when I was a kid, so while everyone wanted to have the "Fab Four" get back together, I was infatuated with the idea of C,S,N and Y getting back together. Neil Young was always the hold out, which probably propelled my desire all the more.

The impresario and consummate San Francisco Band promoter Bill Graham had just died in a helicopter crash flying home from a Huey Lewis (who years later I would meet) and the News concert. A week later Graham's eponymous company BGP put on a huge celebration in his honor dubbed "Laughter, Love and Music" in Golden Gate Park on Sunday November 3, 1991. The turnout at the Polo Fields was amazing and I was lucky enough to be one of them. A 'who's who" of headliners performed as an homage and thank you to Bill, including Carlos Santana, Jackson Brown, John Fogarty, Journey, Robin Williams, the Grateful Dead and yes! The "Four Horseman": Crosby, Stills, Nash AND Young! Life was complete! Well maybe not complete, but I was *thrilled!*

Two days later, I had an appointment with the Chef Owner of the Mountain House Restaurant in Redwood City. I had been trying for several months to get this appointment with the Chef to re-write his entire wine list and today was finally *the* day. We were going to spend all afternoon on it and I was going to be a hero for getting the lion's share of this very prestigious wine list, after all this time.

I drove up the very steep hillside, ascending above the Bay Area skyline loaded for bear. I had 2 cases of wine samples for him to try. Overkill perhaps, but this appointment was a long time coming, almost a year in fact and I was determined to close the deal. I got out of my car sporting a 3-piece suit, put on my suit coat, straightened my collar and tie, grabbed my bags of wines and started heading for the door when the Chef walked out.

"Can't meet with you today."

"What?! But I have all the wines we talked about."

"Can't meet with you today."

(I was starting to feel somewhere between annoyed and enraged.) "I even have the sample covers for the wine menus."

"Sorry. I can't meet with you today."

I was trying to keep my cool. I looked down the hallway to the Fourier and saw a wild-eyed, scraggly haired dude on the phone.

"Is that Neil Young?" I asked.

"That's why I can't meet with you today."

"Ok...but, when he gets off the phone, would you introduce us please?"

Somewhat reluctantly he agreed.

So here I am in my 3-piece suit, meeting Neil Young and telling him about how his songs influenced me, that he was my hero-he was my chosen Poet and thanked him profusely for getting back together with David, Graham and Steven just a couple of days ago. Neil looked me up in down as he was giving me a "fish" handshake, looking incredulously that I should be one of his biggest fans.

That night at the Mountain House they recorded the album "Harvest Moon".

12

Sonoma Ambassador

My wife and I had always intended to move to Sonoma and settle in before retiring and ease on into the "Wine Country Lifestyle", but when 911 happened, it decimated our high tech Venture Catalyst firm, Inter*Net*ionalExpertise (i.e., IE) as well as the Twin Towers in New York and the Pentagon in D.C.- 5 miles from where I grew up.

On that perilous day, I learned that I had indirectly saved one of my clients' lives:

Nelson Cicchittio, founder and original CEO of Avatier. I had arranged a meeting for the Chairman of the Board and a finalist candidate to be the new CEO to meet in New York, as the Company was growing fast and getting too big for Nelson who is a very bright guy, but lacking time and experience in the most critical role at a crucial time in the Company's projected growth. The candidate was flying from Washington D. C. to meet the Chairman in NYC on September 11, 2001. Nelson pleaded with me to be a part of that meeting and I talked him out of it.

"But I already have my roundtrip plane ticket to New York and back to the Bay Area".

"Let's just see how this meeting goes between them and if all goes well, we'll set a meeting with all three of you-that would be much more appropriate and best use of everyone's time," I said.

"Well, ok, I guess", Nelson responded reluctantly. "If you really think that's best."

"That's what you're paying me for. It would just change the dynamics too much. Believe me."

"Oh, ok."

On that fateful morning, I got a call from Nelson.

"Jesus, Sandrew. You saved my life! I was supposed to be on United Flight 93!!!

-*you know*, the one that crashed in that Pennsylvania field. Holy Shit! Thanks, man."

And that's what put me right back into the wine business for the second time.

I always thought of myself as an Ambassador for Sonoma. Napa didn't need the help, anymore. I started in Napa and will probably finish in Napa. When I started selling wine in Colorado and California on the wholesale side, I always felt the need to tell the Sonoma story to help build the momentum, prestige and prosperity that Napa had gained in recognition. It was just a matter of time and conviction. I was fortunate enough to be there in the early days for Iron Horse Vineyards, Matansas Creek, Lyeth, Dehlinger and to be part of the launch teams for Mazzocco, Gloria Ferrer, DeLormier, Viansa, B.R.Cohn, Schug, Merry Vintners (Merry Edwards), and Arrowood.

Now it was time to help with the next gen of wineries. Having been out of the wine business for some years, I never let myself get "rusty". I read Wine Spectator, Wine Advocate, Connoisseur's Guide, some Steven Tanzer (Wine Enthusiast and Vinous were not established yet and James Suckling and Jim Gordon were still with Wine Spectator then). I went to several wine tastings offered throughout the Bay Area and stayed in touch with my top retail and restaurant accounts. I was still *very* passionate about it and being a part of it, as one of the folks behind the scenes. With all that I had learned from my High Tech experience and launching companies like Netscape, Quote.com, Excite! and dozens of others, I felt like I had a pretty good handle on business-*anybody's business*. So I became a business consultant-this time for the wine industry.

I kept my palate in check too, by hosting blind tastings with our wine group, "The Grapenuts". (I always challenged everybody to come up with a better name,'cause even though I started it, I didn't like it, so I kinda put it out there so they wouldn't like it and come up with something better-they never did, so here I am writing about it decades later and the name remains.) I also frequently would go winetasting in Napa, Sonoma, San Luis Opisbo, Monterey, Mendocino and Santa Barbara to stay connected, be in touch and not get "rusty". I noticed that all too often, folks in the various tasting rooms would often be asked questions where they would get stumped. It seemed like they were always slow to answer and would be silently hoping that if they s-l-o-w-l-y turned around that eventually, the winemaker would pop out of the back room, into the Tasting Room and magically appear, seamlessly answering the question without a hiccup. (No pun intended here!)

Sonoma Ambassador

AHA! There is a need! These kind and well-intentioned tasting room associates, knew their script from what they had been instructed to say, but take them off script; *well there's an opportunity!* There was a hole. There was a need. Tom Mazzocco, owner of Mazzocco winery and Vineyards told me he was inspired as an 8 year old driving with his Dad behind a cement mixer. It had a bumper sticker that read: "*Find a hole and fill it*". He reinterpreted it to: "Find a <u>need</u> and fill it."

Dr. Mazzocco invented the foldable IOL, a foldable silicone lens (the "Mazzocco Taco"), a <u>major</u> breakthrough for Cataract surgery in the mid 1980's. He is also a pilot and a golfer. His practice was in LA, but his winery in Sonoma, across from the Healdsburg airport. His golf clubs would not fit into his Cessna, so what was he to do? Why of course, he invented the collapsible golf club! Remarkable man, gracious man. Generous man. One night in early 1986, he opened up his cellar for us-anything was fair game-*anything*! Out came the vaunted 1982's Petrus, Chateau Latour and Haut Brion. *THANK YOU TOM!* One rarely gets a treat like that and he made no bones about it.

So I adopted his philosophy. I would take that 'hole' of a need for more wine education and history in the Tasting Rooms and fill it. After all, I'm a bit of a

California Wine historian-mainly because I grew up in the golden era of it and, *ok*, because I'm a wine geek.

And thus, the birth of Sandrew's Wine Services: Private Chef and Personal Sommelier

"Delivering the ultimate California wine experience!"

We can tailor-make any program designed especially for and by you to make a once–in-a-lifetime experience! Including "vertical", "horizontal", "intersectional" and blind tastings.

Food and Wine pairing with Seminar:
- Wine consultation with Client, Food pairing and recommendations and coordination with Chef
- Wine procurement and delivery
- Presentations and service of wines, historical notes, and flavor profiles
- Explanation of the "whys" and "how tos" of pairings
- Wine Education: in depth interactive seminar .Discussions include world class wines and specific focus on California wines, history, origins, how to taste like a professional, terminology, flavor spectrums, "balance", "terroir", microclimates, where do those flavors come from? Q and A
- Food and Wine pairing:
- Wine consultation, Food pairing and recommendations and coordination with Chef
- Wine procurement and delivery
- Service of wines with appropriate dishes/appetizers, historical notes, and flavor profiles
- Explanation of the "whys" and "how tos" of pairings

Wine Seminar:
- Wine consultation with Client
- Wine procurement and delivery
- Presentations of wines, historical notes, and flavor profiles
- Wine Education: in depth interactive seminar .Discussions include world class wines and specific focus on California wines, history, origins, how to taste like a professional, terminology, flavor spectrums, "balance", "terroir", microclimates, where do those flavors come from? Q and A

This became my Renaissance period. I was pitching and providing my consulting services, creating and conducting Wine and Food pairings to Napa and Sonoma wineries and to the private sector, writing for Vine Times magazine, Chairman of the Board for The Villages of Valley of the Moon (Kenwood and Glen Ellen), growing my own, part time Associate in Benziger's tasting room, managing a rental condo in Kauai, playing Jack London and Santa Claus as well as being an extra in 2 movies. *That is to say, I was trying to endure mid-life crisis, the Great Recession and the Financial Crisis as best I could!*

So now here we are, living in Sonoma County in the little hamlet of Glen Ellen, having moved from Marin County, home of the Redwood Hot Tubers and Chardonnay drinkers. If you ever get a chance to see the movie, "The Serial" starring Martin Mull and my friend and Glen Ellen neighbor, Tommy Smothers, you'll know what I mean! It's stereotypically hilarious.

Here's a reprint from one of my Vine Times articles:

Winemaker Profile: Michael Muscardini

Michael Muscardini is the quintessential Sonoma Winemaker: he's Italian, down -to-earth and extremely passionate about his craft." Bottled with love for the joy of living" is embossed on every bottle of the less than 3,000 case total production. This phrase, coined by wife Robyn, embodies the spirit that is Muscardini Cellars, voted "Best Micro Winery" for reds at the California State Fair.

It's a classic story starting with Michael's Grandfather, Emilio Alchera, who was born in the village of Calliano, just outside of the city of Asti in the Piemonte region of Italy. Emilio came to America in 1909 via Ellis Island in New York. then heading to the West Coast by train to meet his two brothers, Antonio and Louis, whereupon he settled in San Francisco and owned some corner grocery stores, until he opened St. Helena Napa Wine company, where he gladly poured his homemade wine from the barrel right into the jug for his customers. There is a great picture in the tasting room depicting this rich tradition that carries on at 8910 Sonoma Highway Kenwood, California. Here you can also taste the wines of buddy and fellow Vintner, Ty Caton. (Editor's note: This is no longer the case)

"My goal here is to make food-friendly wines that have a strong fruit component to them", says the affable Muscardini. I can attest to this, having conducted a Food and Wine pairing for a sold out crowd last year. "We specialize in Sangiovese, Syrah, Barbera and my flagship wine 'Tesoro', which is a proprietary blend of Sangiovese, Cabernet (Sauvignon) and Syrah." And quite frankly, absolutely delicious!

Michael is not only Winemaker and Marketer for his own brand, but is quite active in the wine community, serving as President of The Sonoma Valley Vintners and Growers Alliance (SVVGA) for the second year in a row, but he will always make time for customers, as I witnessed firsthand. We had just finished our interview and he was literally out the door and heading down highway 12 when he got a call from 2 couples from Texas. He promptly turned around and came back to personally serve his repeat guests who had met him last year and loved the wines-very impressive! "You just don't get service like this anymore. Most wineries are too big or don't care about giving you this kind of attention" remarked one of the Texans. "That's why we come back!" Indeed!

If you would like Michael to take you through his award winning wines, you can usually find him there on the weekends or make a private appointment to taste "Upstairs". You can contact him through the website: www.MuscardiniCellars.com You can also find out about many scheduled events, including my next Food and Wine Pairing there!

Here's my take on the wines:

2009 Rosato di Sangiovese: (bone dry)
Nose: Blood Orange peel and ripe wild strawberry with earthy, mineral accents
Palate: Watermelon and rose pedal finish

2007 Sangiovese "Pauli Ranch": Double Gold, Best of Class!
Nose: Toasty Oak, vanilla, plum, pomegranate, potpourri spice, mint, roasted coffee and anise
Palate: Blackberry, red and black plums, sage, black pepper and orange pekoe tea, velvety tannins and great color
2008 Barbera "Ukia Valley", Mendocino:

Nose: Blueberry, blueberry pie filling, violets, vanilla, cedar, sandalwood
Palate: Red plum, pomegranate and blackberry liqueur

2007 Syrah "Gracie Creek" Sonoma Valley: Double gold-Best of Class, SF Chronicle competition!

Cool climate syrah that only yields 2 tons per acre

Nose: Big tannins give way to violets black plum, perfume, cardamom, red delicious apple skin and cedar

Palate: Black Plum, blackberry preserve, white pepper and spice rack

2007 "Tesoro" (Cal/Ital Super Tuscan):

Nose: Smoke, toast, mocha, raspberry, cassis and Asian spices

Palate: Plum, raspberry and spice box-very smooth finish with all components well integrated and in balance

My favorite part of my "Sandrew's Wine Services" business was my Private Chef, Personal Sommelier programs-Wine and Food pairings of course!

Here's what we did for Michael Muscardini:

<u>Muscardini Cellars Educational Event 7/22/10</u>

Dancing Somm

2009 Rosato di Sangiovese Monte Rosso, paired with
Prosciutto wrapped fresh local Cantaloupe melon

2008 Barbera Mendocino, paired with
Vine-smoked, dry-rubbed Baby Back Ribs in Blueberry Balsamic reduction

2008 Sangiovese Monte Rosso paired with
Sautéed mushroom cap stuffed with house made Kalamata Tapenade

2007 "Tesoro" Super Tuscan Monte Rosso, paired with
Grilled double secret herb-encrusted Sonoma Lamb in Rosemary aujus

---

Here's a personalized menu I created and cooked for Jonathan Maack:

August 11, 2009
A VERY SPECIAL EVENING
FOR JAEL AND JONATHAN MAACK

—

Dungeness Crab taragon Dijonaise paired with Iron Horse Vineyards Brut "Green Valley" 2006

Caprese Salad of local Heirloom tomatoes, fresh basil, and Laurel Chenel goat cheese w/BR Cohn Olive oil and Lambert Bridge Viognier "Alexander Valley" 2007

Pan-seared Sea scallop on a bed of caraway, fennel and Gravenstien Apples paired with Signatera "Sangiacomo Vineyards" Chardonnay Carneros 2007

Caggiano Italian Sausage (Carneros) served with Grilled curried Sonoma baby eggplant and summer squash

A.Rafanelli Zinfandel "Dry Creek" 1998

Sonoma Ambassador

Petaluma Duck Confit with Gran Marnier Bing Cherry, Chinese five spice "marmalade" beside green lentils, baby carrots and torpedo onions

Merry Edwards Pinot Noir "Russian River" 2007

Piece de Resistance:

Chocolate Truffles

St.Francis "Sonoma Valley" Port 2005

Sandrew, the Original Personal Sommelier

decadence, with a personally selected "tour" of Sonoma wines paired with Chef Adair's regional organic cuisine!

Iron Horse 2005 "Wedding Cuvee" Green Valley

Point Reyes Blue Cheese and Grilled Pear Tartlet
Lambert Bridge 2007 Viognier Knights Valley

Avocado and Grilled Shrimp Salad
Avocado on a bed of fresh hearts of romaine topped with lemon and shallot grilled prawns and a sweet pepper coulis
Stuhlmuller 2006 Reserve Chardonnay Alexander Valley

Grilled Salmon with Raviolis in cream sauce
Salmon on a bed of raviolis with chanterelles, fresh ricotta and a smoky tomato-tarragon cream sauce
Pappapietro Perry 2006 Pinot Noir Russian River

Braised Short Ribs or Grilled Asparagus
With a peppery Parmesana-Reggiano risotto, zinfandel and veal demi glace winter vegetables.

Pappapietro Perry 2006 Sonoma Coast
(from Magnum)

Dark Chocolate Torte Decadence
With blueberry reduction and ganache
St. Francis 2005 "Port" Sonoma Valley

Sonoma Ambassador

Here's another one of my articles during my Renaissance period and the menu I cooked up for Enkidu's Wine Club Members:

Enkidu

Enkidu's Tasting room is situated in a small shopping center, *The Kenwood Village at an unassuming location indeed, considering it sports such "Big Wines". Owner / Winemaker, Phil Staehle is as driven and passionate about winemaking as any I have ever met. His path to becoming a Winery Proprietor was not immediately eminent. "I was recruited to U.C. Davis to pitch for their baseball team. My major was Law, not enology or viticulture", chuckles the ebullient Staehle. Phil recalls his first wine was a Charles Krug Grey Riesling, then "Cold Duck". But his inspiration came from a 1975 Barolo. "I had a 50 to 60 bottle collection of wine in college".

After college, Phil managed the Bar and was the Wine Director for Skates Restaurant on the water in the East Bay. His next opportunity came to be Assistant Winemaker for Carmenet, part of the Chalone Group, where he met the late Dick Graph, a legend in his own right. "Dick had vision, and I really learned that from him. Pam Starr - she's such a great winemaker, also became a mentor as did Jeff Baker. Jeff's style was about discussion and consensus. His attention to detail is very focused and his experimentation really helped me to broaden my horizons.

The name "Enkidu" comes from one of the oldest stories ever recorded: *The Epic of Gilgamesh.* Written in Sumerian cuneiform nearly 4500 years ago, the story details the life of King Gilgamesh and his best friend Enkidu. Enkidu was a steward of the land and protector of animals, and was created by the gods as a foil to Gilgamesh. Two-thirds deity and one-third human, he embodied strength, passion, and incredible bravery, yet at times showed fear and trepidation of the unknown. Early in his existence, Enkidu was rustic and rough around the edges, and over time he became more cultured and refined. While Enkidu's character contained some imperfections, he did evolve while staying true to his nature. This can also be said of wine. The winery takes direction from the character of Enkidu, looking inward and adhering to beliefs which guide our efforts.

Phil, a Lake County native, does not own any grapes, but has long term contracts with vineyards in Sonoma, Napa and Lake Counties. "They let me control it!" says the affable Staehle. If you are looking for a unique, uncrowded tasting room experience with wonderfully delicious, balanced white wines & big Reds, then Enkidu is a must. (It doesn't hurt in these economic times that the wines are very reasonably – make that under priced). For more information go to www.EndiduWine.com or call me for an extremely personalized tour.

(* note: no longer; now in Sonoma Square)

Enkidu Food and Wine Pairing
October 8th, 2009

Kick Ranch Sauvignon Blanc - Sonoma County 2008
Endive stuffed with Crab rolled in a Tarragon Dijonaise

Kiamberell's Pinot Noir - Russian River Valley 2007
Petaluma Duck Breast Confit topped with Grand Marnier infused Montmorency cherries sprinkled with Chinese Five Spice

Bedrock Zinfandel (120 year old vines!) - Sonoma Valley 2008
Grilled Dry Rubbed Baby back Ribs accompanied with Hoisin/ Boysenberry Sauce

Odyssey Syrah - Russian River Valley 2006
Cabernet Vine Smoked Herb Crusted New Zealand Leg O' Lamb in Rosemary Jus

"Amuse Bouche" Sautéed Mushroom Cap filled with House made Kalamata Olive Tapenade to be paired with Guests' Choice of Enkidu Wine

Please join us after for a special late night tasting.

All wine purchases discounted 20% for guests.

Sonoma Ambassador

While living in Glen Ellen, Sonoma, home to famed writer, vintner, entrepreneur, innovator and long before his time Hippie and liberal activist on the the Berkely bully pulpit starting the free speech movement, Jack London, I was asked to play the iconic Jack. (I think mostly because of my brown leather jacket.) A part of why Kat and I moved there was hoping I would get inspiration with the spirit of London as my muse. (We'll see how well *this* book does as testament!) The Glen Ellen parade is always in October, probably the most

beautiful time to visit wine country with all the vineyards' Fall colors in full glory, and it travels all of both blocks of the tiny village. It's quite the Americana experience and fun for all.

I would don my Leather Jacket, muss up my hair and read from London's "Call of the Wild", read a snippet or two, get about five steps, look up from the book and look left and right shouting out to the crowd:
"If you don't know Glen Ellen, you don't know jack!"

There was always a table or two of local wines and 2 of the Saloons Jack frequented and people manning those booths and taverns would call me over saying "Come on have a drink. Jack would!"

At the time, I was the National Sales Manager and Kat was the Assistant Manager for the little tasting room in town for Sullivan-Birney Vineyards and Winery based on Sonoma Mountain. Our Winemaker was Rolando Herrea, a fantastic winemaker in his own right with his Mi Sueno (My Dream) and protégé of Paul Hobbs. On the 100th anniversary of "Call of the Wild", there were many celebrations and readings throughout the County-in Santa Rosa, Sonoma and even up on London Ranch (Jack's home turned Park with the Jack London Vineyards now produced by Kenwood Winery). Kat had a great idea for that special day. Why don't we do a special wine tasting that includes a reading from the book in the tasting room? Because Sullivan-Birney doesn't charge for tastings, they would charge that day and all proceeds would go to the doggie park (Liz Perone) to benefit them since the story is written from the viewpoint of Buck, the dog turned wolf, an allegory of Jack London himself. "It's a triple win for everybody!" Kat exclaimed.

But who would play Jack?

Well now, that little reading of an excerpt turned into a performance. Forty-five minutes worth! Even though we were a late entry, we ended up being the front page of the Press Democrat newspaper the next day. Kat dressed in some vintage clothing, as Charmian London, there was Miles, a huge black German Shepard as "Buck" and I guess I just *had to* reprise my role with my brown leather jacket.

about your marketing expertise and would like to talk to you about that."

Rather generic name. I don't know any Mike Brown. I kinda forgot about it for a couple of weeks, but that's not professional and certainly not like me. So I called this newbee back and left him a voice mail. Didn't hear back from him for a couple of weeks and then had a voice mail:

"Hi Sandrew. It's Michael Browne from Kosta Browne getting back to you. Sorry but I lost my phone. But in the meantime, Parker just rated my Pinot 96 points, so I don't need your help anymore. Thanks."

Just shoot me right now! UGGGGHHHH! Kosta Browne?! Really?

Another rock star winemaker based in Sonoma is Erich Bradley, of Sojourn Cellars, Pangloss Cellars and Repris wines. Erich and I first met when he was winemaker at Audelssa. One of the most unpretentious souls (let alone winemakers) you'll ever meet. Audelssa had taken over our Sullivan Birney tasting room spot in Glen Ellen. The fruit was coming from the Sonoma side of the Mayacamas and Erich put his magic touch on those beauties. There was a point in time when Robert Parker would only taste Bradley's wines in Sonoma Valley; but *he'll* never tell you that.

On Kat's 60th birthday, I wanted to make it extra special for the big event, so I rented the biggest place Nick's at the Cove in Tomales Bay had to offer. I had Jeff Kunde and Mike Benziger sign 3 liter bottles of their respective reserve cabernets for the occasion. We had many more bottles that night with all of our guests and we sang Chuck Berry's "Sweet Lil' Sixteen" and changed the lyrics to Sweet lil' Six-tee, and San Francisco Bay changed to Tamales Bay, while the Rolling Stones accompanied us on DVD. Later that night we went in to the restaurant to have a late dinner and cake, when a bottle of Champagne showed up at our table.

"Compliments of the gentleman in the corner", our server informed us, placing down champagne flutes on the table. Turning around in both directions in the dimly lit restaurant, we caught a glimpse of the generous patron-it was Erich, raising a glass: "Happy Birthday, Kat!"
What a helluva guy!

Sonoma Ambassador

As I took on the self-appointed role of the Sonoma Ambassador, I took it to an even more specified level, creating VAVOOM! "Villages Association of Valley Of the Moon" to establish a comprehensive and cohesive marketing organization to create awareness for all of the small businesses in Glen Ellen and Kenwood Villages.

("Valley of the Moon" is another Jack London book and what the Miwok Indian Tribe called the corridor we now know as Sonoma Highway 12, between the Mayacamas and Sonoma Mountain Ranges, where it is said you can see the moon rise and fall at least 7 times during the full moon night.)

At the Jack London Village shopping center, where several of the businesses including restaurants, a chocolatier, cheese monger, artists and wine tasting rooms resided, we had a big Christmas/Holiday shindig where I played Santa Claus for the kids. I had to volunteer myself, as no one else was willing to don the suit! But it was fun and we brought people from all around the Bay Area, creating good will, exposure, revenue and awareness for the tiny little hamlet.

On My 50th Birthday, we had an intimate group celebrating with winery owners/winemakers Pricsilla and David Cohen of Moondance Cellars, Lauren and John Wetzel of Alexander Valley Vineyards and Nick Brown of Jeep Tours at the famous Girl and the Fig's sister restaurant, Fig Café right in the heart of Glen Ellen. Multiple bottles of local wine were being passed around the table and as we were enjoying ourselves, there was a rather big and boisterous gentlemen wearing jeans and a white T-shirt. The "white" T-shirt was covered on the front with multiple purpleblue, wine-stained hand prints; the sign of a true winemaker.

"Oh I gotta know *this* guy!" I said to the table and promptly got up to meet him.

"Hey, man, I don't know who you are, but with a shirt like that, I figure I better know you!" I extended my hand.

"Russel Bevan!" he said with a firm grip and voice.

"Sandrew Montgomery! Nice to meet you. You in the wine business?"

"You could say that."

"Who are you with?"

"I make a little wine for myself and Three Sticks."

"Nice." I replied. Well I better get back to my table-great to meet you!"

Within a few minutes, mostly full bottles of Mollydooker Carnival of Love Shiraz and Sine Qua Non were hand delivered by the larger than life Russel to our table. "Really? Thanks Man!"

"Happy Birthday!"

We've been friends ever since and he has gone on to make some of California's highest rated wines for Showket, Chase Cellars, Chateau Boswell and his own Bevan Cellars.

Tommy Smothers of the famed comedy team, The Smothers Brothers with his brother ("Mom always liked you best") Dickey, were the ones who discovered Steve Martin. You may know that, but you probably didn't know that Tommy is also a winemaker and has his own label, "Remick Ridge". He and Dick Arrowood of Chateau St. Jean, Arrowood and Amapola Creek fame made the wine together. Tommy was my neighbor and friend when we lived in Glen Ellen in Sonoma County. Tommy is a great guy and always the comedian. And, yes, he's still the world's greatest yo-yo trickster! He was the one who came up with the quip "Sonoma is for wine, Napa is for auto parts".

Tommy is the one who dubbed me the "Dancing Sommelier". Having been to a few parties at his home, I always loved and admired this picture in his living room of him and John Lennon on the day they sat on the bed, sang and recorded "Give Peace a Chance". For some reason, I was too shy to ask him for a pic. After all these years, one day I finally worked up the nerve to ask him if we could take a picture together, holding that historic photograph.

"Hey Tommy-would you mind if Kat took a picture of you and me holding that picture of you and Lennon?"

"Nope." Tommy was quick to respond.

"Oh, I'm sorry, man. I didn't mean to offend you."

"No, it's not that. I just gave it away a couple of weeks ago."

"Damn!" I thought to myself. "Oh, I waited *too long*!"

Sensing the disappointment on my face, Tommy said "Wait a minute", and abruptly left the room. He headed down the hall to his bedroom and came back smiling and said, "How's this?"

So we took *this* picture together.

The Dancing Sommelier, Tommy Smothers, Tommy, John Lennon and Yoko Ono.

Damn it Yoko! Once again, you got in the middle of another great thing!

"Diversitile"-moment of genius?

I have personally trained several hundreds of Restaurant and Tasting Room personnel over the years.

Being a foodie, I have always had a passion for Wine and Food pairings and a special love affair with Pinot Noir. One day in San Diego I was teaching the servers of Café Pacifica and was taking questions. A bright female server posed to me a hypothetical question:

"What if it's Saturday night, I just clocked in and my station had already been triple sat. So now I'm already in the weeds before getting the night started. Everybody is ordering different entrees and I'm *freakin' out*. What would you do?"

"Don't pull you hair out" I retorted. "That's a great question and everybody has that nightmarish dream. I'm guessing this actually happened to you?"

"Well yes! So what should I have done?"

"Easy! Sauvignon Blanc for the white, Pinot Noir for the red."

And that's when I either had a moment of genius-or, I was slurring my words!

"Pinot Noir is 'diversitle'! It's *SO* diverse, *SO* versatile try and miss-match it with food. Yes it's redundant, but that's the point I'm trying to drive home." I said with such confidence.

And that's when I coined the word, "diversitile" and have been using it ever since.

I love Pinot Noir so much, I wrote an "Ode to Pinot" as an homage.

Armando Ceja (Ceja Vineyards) and Bruce Rector (Ahh Winery and Glen Ellen/Benziger) wanted to help save the Arts programs for local schools in Sonoma. They threw a fundraiser to create awareness and raise money. They called it "Vida, Vino, Y Poeta".

A great event held on a classically beautiful, sunny Carneros day in some friend's vineyards.

The wine was flowing, kids were having tons of fun, the auction was raising the funds needed and there were several poets, both professional and amateur. I tossed my poem into the amateur ring and had great success (not to mention most importantly luck!)

Sonoma Ambassador

Ode to Pinot
By Sandrew Montgomery
Poetry Winner at Vida, Vino, Y Poeta's

NWAH!...
AHHhhh...

That finicky little grape
That gives all winemakers a fit.
And to wit,
Makes them want to say
"Oh Sh_ _!
To hell with it!"

I mean to wax the poetic prophetic
Of the likes of Ipson,
But I feel more
Like Henry ... Gibson.

Flavors elegant and broad in style,
Tremendously nuanced in its profile
That I, as an Oenophile,
Coined it, "DIVERSITILE."

It makes me merry,
Especially, when reminiscent of bing cherry.
It begets mirth
With scents of violets and earth,
Clove and cinnamon spice,
Paired with sautéed wild mushrooms,
Oh! —So —Nice!

From Burgundy to Santa Lucia,
Willamette to Santa Maria,
Russian River and Sonoma Coast,
And of course, right here in Carneros.
No other varietal can seduce,
Like the noble grape of Eros!

Pinot Passion, The Benzigers, Biodynamic Farming Practices and More

When Kat and I moved to Glen Ellen, I had no idea that one day I would be working for the Benziger Family. Back in Colorado, I had been competing for years with their "Fighting Varietals" category of wines that they created with their Glen Ellen Brand. Here I was living just 1.6 miles away from their winery and tasting room. I guess it was inevitable. And I'm glad it was.

Now Patriarch, Mike Benziger, who started the Glen Ellen Winery by convincing his Dad Bruno to leave their very successful New York wine shop and come to California to start a new venture in 1973. In 1980, the Benzigers bought the historic Wegener Ranch, just below Jack London's Ranch on Sonoma Mountain, a former Hippie Commune for 10 years in the 70's, turned Vineyards in the 80's. They became Demeter Certified Biodynamic in 2000 with the help of Biodynamic Consultant Alan York, who then helped Sting create his Biodynamic Vineyards and Winery in Italy.

Mike once told me of the commune, pointing out "the Cabernet was all over here, the cannabis, all over there."

"What happened to all the cannabis?" I asked.

He simply replied nonchalantly, "We smoked it all!"

Mike Benziger is one of the most charismatic fellas you will ever meet.

I consider him a mentor, as his enthusiasm and passion for wine and life itself is virtually unparalleled. His energy and leadership for the Family, the Family business and California wine as a world class leader is on a parallel of another one of my mentors, Robert Mondavi. I want to thank Mike from the bottom of my heart for the opportunity to work with him and *all* the Benzigers (Bob, Joe, Patsy, her husband Todd, Kathy and Chris). He gave me the opportunity to assist

Pinot Passion, The Benzigers, Biodynamic Farming Practices and More

with the creation of the Pinot Passion Parlor, a pet project of his as a true foray into Pinot Noir as a serious part of the Benziger portfolio.

With the help of the late Alan York as consultant, the Benzigers decided to go as organic as you can get: Demeter Certified. This is the highest form of organic farming, originally devised by Rudolf Steiner in his native country Austria in 1924. Mike took me under his wing and taught me all about it. From the insectories, to the sheep who graze between the rows and simultaneously till the land and fertilize to the 9 kinds of composting, including the Scottish Hereford cows who, as Mike says, "Lay the golden turds", to the raptors (Hawks, Falcons etc.) who fly above and scare away the Starlings and other berry eating flying pests to the silica in the cow horns and their burial at the right cycles of the

Gold Ridge Sandstone
Geologically young, lithified sand and fossilized shells, found only in western Sonoma County.
Pastorale and Quarter Moon Vineyards

moon. I attended some of those Moon Cycle ceremonies and my favorite one has to be when the youngest two second generation Benzigers had a little sibling play. Kathy was wearing some rather nice shoes while standing above the pit that Chris had just dug for the ceremonial burial. Her shoe fell off and into the pit and she kindly asked Chris to pull it out. Of course being the younger brother he promptly proceeded to bury the shoe even deeper, shoveling more dirt on top!

Mike taught me the whole of this holistic approach to wine growing so well, I taught the class on Biodynamic farming practices at The Napa Valley College, where I also taught the class on 'Clones'. I guess I am truly a wine geek, after all, because if you're not really into these 2 topics, your eyes will surely glaze over or you will revert to texting!

So I helped Mike and the Benzigers create the "Pinot Passion Parlor". We started this in the original farm house that the Benzigers moved into on Halloween night. The rains came through the leaky old roof into the living room where the kids were all sleeping on the floor. I'm sure these sophisticated New Yorkers were collectively ecstatic about this new venture out west with this kind of start!

The Pinot Passion Parlor features the entire array of Pinot Noirs produced with a screen projecting the virtual vineyard tours of De Coelo (Sonoma Coast) and Bella Luna (Russian River). We had soil types on display, including the coveted "Goldridge Sandstone dust", found only in one place around the *entire* world: Western Sonoma County. Basically fossils fused together with sand, making for the perfect drainage to produce tiny berries, creating fantastic Pinot Noir fruit!

Being in charge of this new experience for the family was very exciting for me and really got my juices flowing (so to speak!). While not conducting the Pinot Passion Parlor tastings, I was also a tour guide for the VIP Biodynamic Tram Tours and host for the Cave Seated Tastings. Man I had fun 'holding court' in the caves!

Pinot Passion, The Benzigers, Biodynamic Farming Practices and More

In the caves we would taste the current release Reserve Wines including the flagship, Tribute, a tribute in honor of Founder Bruno Benziger.

Unfortunately, the Pinot Passion Parlor was not ADA compliant and we had to close it down and until compliant. While I was at Benziger, I still had my Private Chef, Personal Sommelier business through Sandrews Wine Services and had created one of my Wine and Food pairing experiences in the caves at Kunde for Valentine's Day. I already knew the Kundes fairly well and because it was Spring and therefore hiring season for tasting rooms was about to begin, I applied for one of their positions. My wife was starting with them to help out for Barrel Tasting weekend in March. I worked at both Wineries for a while and was very busy with both, so I started to wind down Sandrews Wine Services. Jeff and Marcia Kunde told me that their "Wildwood Room" was only being used for a Board meeting once a month, and I could see a bit of anguish in the mild mannered Jeff's face.

"Why not create a wine and food experience here to show off their Reserve wines and take advantage of this prime Real Estate?" I thought to myself? So I proposed it to them and their TR Manager Dick Perman. They embraced the idea. "I'll even write you a business plan for it!"

So, it was time for me to move on to Kunde exclusively and say a sad, but joyous farewell to the Benzigers.

CHEERS!

Proud Grand Daddy Mike in the middle, flanked by brother Bob to the far left, sisters Kathy and Patsy, brother Joe to the far right.

Love you guys!

Paintball Wars
(not quite " the Hatfields and McCoys")

Living in the tiny hamlet of Glen Ellen, it's always easy to visit the next door Village of Kenwood, home to Chateau St. Jean, St. Francis, Kenwood Winery and Kunde Family Winery. All of these wineries have tasting rooms and are all situated along the stretch that is Sonoma Highway 12, butted up on the westside of the Mayacamas Mountains. It should be noted that all of these properties somehow miraculously survived the horrendous and apocalyptic Firestorm of October 2017.

I had frequented all of these tasting rooms on many occasions and was even a wholesale rep for Chateau St. Jean, back in the eighties. As "Sandrew, the Original Personal Sommelier" I offered (read: "solicited") my services to the Kunde family and they hired me to do a wine and food pairing for their Wine Club members for Valentine's Day in their caves that are prominently featured in Bottle Shock. (In fact, 75% of the movie was filmed throughout the 1,850 contiguous acre property.) As a writer for Vine Times magazine www.vinetimes.com I wrote an article about the Fifth generation growers and vintners.

Apparently the Valentine's pairing was quite a success and eventually they hired me to create and conduct their wine and food pairing program amongst other things.

Kunde Wildwood Food and Wine Experience
Redwood Hills Chevre with Black Mission Fig and Walnut Tapenade
Sauvignon Blanc "Block SB 20" 2010 Retail: $21.00 Club: $16.80

Paintball Wars

Cremini Mushroom and Matos St George Turnover
Reserve Zinfandel "Century Vines" 2008 Retail: $35.00 Club: $28.00

Thai BBQ Pork Tostado with Jicama Slaw
"Red Dirt Red" Proprietary Blend 2008 Retail: $28.00 Club: $22.40

Braised Beef Short Ribs with Truffle Oil
Cabernet Sauvignon "Drummond Vineyard" 2008 Retail: $35 Club: $28

Polenta Bars with Tart Cherry and Point Reyes Blue
Reserve Cabernet Sauvignon 2009   Retail: $45.00 Club: $37.00

One of those other duties was conducting Mountain Top tours; a Reserve tasting at a 1400 foot elevation. On one occasion, while my guests were enjoying their Kunde reserve wines, "Maestro" (a movie about legendary wine consultant Andre Tchelistcheff) was being filmed by helicopter (just like in Bottle Shock) over these 1,850 contiguous acres, the pilot decide he would buzz us. The helicopter blades were whippin' up quite breeze. I turned around and said to my guests: "Oh look. You have white caps in your wine!"

Since it took 20 minutes to get to the destination, I would regale stories to guests on the way up and back down the mountain. Some of those stories were about the antics of drinking buddies Louis Kunde and Jack London, the "ambush" by Jim Bundschu (Gundlach Bundschu) and posse on the inaugural Napa Train ride with Richard Branson and the paintball war between the Kundes and Benzigers.

Now they were never *really* the "Hatfields and McCoys", but there was a bit of a sibling rivalry if you will, between the Benzigers and the Kundes. It was all in fun amongst these 2 multi-generational Sonoma Valley families. Their kids went to school together, go on various outings, played on sports teams together and, after all, they were *both* in the wine business.

Every year on Labor Day weekend there is the Sonoma auction. It's a tremendous celebration of Valley life, wine, food, fun, comradery, silliness and it all ends up raising lots of money for the local charities. Sunday is the big auction event.

One year in the brochure, one of the lots up for bid was a Paintball War.

The brochure read something like this:

"Paintball War at the Benziger Estate. All equipment included. Date tbd.
And we bet the Kundes don't have the 'paintballs' to win this auction item!"
Weeeeeeeeell!   Challenge!! (say it French)

Of course, that's all the Kundes needed to be chided with and win that bid!

So before the gavel came down, Jeff Kunde stood up and yelled over to Mike Benziger:

"Just one little thing, Mike."

"What's that Jeff?"

"Well it's not going to be at the Benziger Estate. It's going to be at the Kunde Estate."

"OK, Jeff. Suit yourself", as Mike looked back and winked at all his siblings sitting at the table snickering.

What you need to know is that the Benzigers had *long* been into paintball.

So much so, that they had their own paintball guns, camouflage uniforms- they even had their own paintball *grenades*!

So when that fateful day came around, the Kundes had a family meeting that morning.

"Jeff, what are we gonna do? The Benzigers are SO into this-they're gonna cream us!"

Jeff Kunde responded, "Now hold on a minute. I know they are, and nothing would give me more satisfaction…" Jeff got interrupted-

"But what are we gonna DO??!"

Jeff started to smile ryely and said "Well yaknow, a few days ago I made a phone call to one of my former army guerilla buddies…. (his smile getting bigger) and he subsequently made some phone calls to some of *his* guerilla buddies… and, they will be joining us today!"

As you can imagine there was much laughter and a bit of relief.

5:00 pm was the start time. Both families started to gather 20 minutes before, and Jeff pointed to one side of the road, saying, "You'll be defending that side. We'll be over here."

The clock strikes 5:00 pm and the gun goes off.

The Benzigers begin to approach the Kunde side, spraying paint all along the way, appearing very dominant. The Kundes were standing their ground at first but started to retreat, allowing the Benzigers on their side of the line.

And then, as the Benzigers advanced significantly, *all of a sudden, from behind them, out of the bushes* came the guerilla commandos nailing the Benzigers and beating them at their own game!

After all the commotion started to die down, Chris Benziger, the youngest, just had to get in one more zinger (so to speak):

"Hey Jeff! You know that brand new white truck you just bought?"

"Yeah?" responded Jeff.

"We had one more (paintball) grenade left, so we just *had* to let it go off *inside* your truck!" said Chris with a smart ass smirk and shit-eatin' grin.

Naturally, **all** the Benzigers were laughing raucously.

When the hysterical laughter subsided, Jeff quipped back –"You mean the one that looks just like *your* new white truck?"

"Yeah." Acknowledged Chris.

"Well I just took mine into the shop this morning, so I believe that was your truck *after all*!"

15

Audacious Scandalous Scoundrel

Thomas Jackal* is an ASS. Actually, he is much more than an ASS, more than an ASSHOLE. In my opinion, Thomas Jackal represents everything reprehensible about man. Every despicable trait of mankind's DNA, he embodies. You name it: greed, arrogance, deceit, boldface lies, conniving, scheming, plotting fraud, stealing, intentional misrepresentation, larceny, embezzlement, detrimental denial, reckless regard for repercussion, committing felony after felony and involving innocent others no matter the cost to them. My understanding is he is now in jail or about to be. For the rest of his life. Good on you Vineyard Manager for blowing the whistle! More on that later.

I don't recall who it was that told me I should give Kent Rasmussen a call to consult with him. Kent and his wife Celia Ramsay started their winery back in 1986, crafting what they call "purely poetic Pinot Noir" and the wines are quite yummy. They built a winery on their home property in St. Helena. I called Kent to set up a meeting about my consulting practice and to discuss helping him start his DTC (Direct to Consumer) business. He and Celia were very successful on the wholesale side establishing their brands in fine restaurants and wine shops. But the wine business was changing, the channels of distribution were getting "stuffed" and it was becoming increasingly harder to get the buyers attention to promote your wine-even if they had been loyal in the past, the vast amount of newcomer competition to vie for the buyers' attention, interest and mind share was becoming more than overwhelming.

Cutting out the middle men in the archaic but still vibrant 3-tiered distribution system was becoming increasingly more strategic, as obviously the margins were higher.

Kent accepted my call and made the appointment with me. I pulled into the property and parked alongside some fermentation tanks. I looked around the property from inside my car, asking myself, "Can I see me coming here every day to work?" My gut fast forwarded to the future and I thought "Yeah. This feels right, I *can* see myself pulling into this parking place."

I grabbed my portfolio book and headed out to meet Mr. Rasmussen. There was no signage, so I started walking to the very attractive house.

"Oh no, we won't be meeting up there", came a voice from behind me. "That's my family's house."

"Kent? Hi. I'm Sandrew Montgomery. I'm honored to meet you-I've enjoyed your Pinots for quite some time!"

"Thank you." replied the soft spoken man.

Kent then showed me around the winery. A bit old fashioned, but that was to be expected. We ended up in a small room that served both as lab and conference room. He pointed to a chair by a small table in the small room. "This is our tasting room." I looked around and kept a straight face, because this looked more like a lab than anything.

"Now I see why you need me." I chuckled-*but only a little bit*, as I noticed Kent was expressionless. We had a very pleasant conversation about him and Celia and raising their four children while starting and running a winery and selling the wine themselves. I told him about my background and success in helping launch and build wineries and wine brands like Opus One, Dominus Estate, Rubicon, Forman, Swanson, Sinskey, Signorello, Matansas Creek, Mazzocco and many others and how I would be happy to do the same for him in establishing his tasting room-a *real* Tasting Room. After about 45 minutes of pleasant conversation, I turned to Kent and said: "You really don't want to do this do you?"

"No, I really don't". He responded in a matter of fact way.

"You know you need to do this right?"

"Yeah. Perhaps."

And with that, I stood up. "Alright. Well think about it and let me know. You have my number."

We shook hands, I thanked him for his time and walked back to my car and got in.

"Damn. I really felt like I could see myself coming to work on this property... guess my gut was wrong after all...

Back to Thomas Jackal (*not his real name). A few years later, I got a call from an Executive Head Hunting firm about a great new opportunity in the Napa Valley. It was for a new winery and the owner wanted to open a tasting room. Here was my opportunity to get back to the Napa Valley and even more importantly, to establish myself on the DTC side as a manager and put *all* the different aspects my business consulting practice had afforded me, but this time under one roof. COOL!

The recruiter told me to meet the owner at 10:00 am at the Winery. Now at first, I thought this address was a bit odd.

As I pulled into the property, I pulled alongside those familiar fermentation tanks.

"Hmm! Now isn't this interesting."

I looked around and laughed to myself, "DejaVu!"

This time I was supposed to go up to the "house". I was greeted by a very nice, fairly attractive lady who directed me up the stairs to the office on the right.

A somewhat burly, dark haired man, quite resembling Zac Brown, the Country music star (who it so happened he was big fan of). He pointed to the chair across from his desk and so began the interview. Thomas told me that he had worked for Gallo as an organic vineyard consultant and he now had his own organic vineyard management company where he had over 30 clients in Napa and some in Sonoma as well. As a part of that, he had his own Napa vineyards that he farmed and was making his own wine, different labels at different price points. He and his wife were raising 3 kids and wanted wine to be affordable for them and his Marine Dad, who would otherwise not be able to enjoy Napa wines.

Alright. I buy that. He was very convincing, even a bit charismatic. He told me that he and his wife established this business and were "committed to donating a percentage of every bottle to the ASPCA." (In hindsight I should have been suspicious **then** as he sounded vague and seemed to lack conviction about the percentage -but HEY! I was in an interview for the dream job of a lifetime- so I thought.) I told him I thought that was great because "my wife and I do international animal rescue-well, actually, she does all the work and I just try to take credit for it!"

I winked and we laughed.

"Also", said Thomas, "one percent of our total revenue is donated to environmental causes through the '1% For the Planet' Foundation. "Very Cool." said I.

He told me about all the vineyards he organically farmed and managed for various Napa owners and another 300 acres in Sonoma, somewhere in West

County. His wife always wanted to have a tasting room that she would manage, but, then they had 3 kids. That's why we were talking. Sounded pretty wholesome. Here is this young family, just getting underway with their whole life before them and they were seizing the day and taking care of business.

A couple of days later, I got a call from the Executive Recruiter and she told me "Mr. Jackal would like to make you and offer. Are you available tomorrow at 11:00 am?" "I'll make myself available. In person or by phone?"

"Phone" she said.
"Thank you SO much for presenting me this opportunity."
"Your welcome! Are you excited?"
"Yes, yes I am, but of course, I don't know what the offer is. I'll circle back with you, when he and I get off the phone. Talk to you tomorrow."
And so I accepted.

I started auspiciously on September 11th. Because of the events of Nine Eleven, I was determined that this was instead going to be a good omen. HA! In the beginning, things were good-very good. Thomas gave me the autonomy to create the tasting room in my fashion. I shadowed him for the first 2 days and listened to his stories with the few guests we had. In between guests, I was writing the business plan which would become the strategy and standard operating procedures for years to come. Man, I was in my comfort zone. Devising a high level business plan and model when not engaging, entertaining guests, selling them wine and signing them up for our brand new wine club. Exciting!

It went on like this for a few months and I had this young man who would visit our tasting room once a week. He was in the tasting room at Charles Krug, not far from our tasting room and winery and he kept bugging me for a job. I thought 'yeah, I like this kid. He's smart, can help me out with social media and other technical aspects and pour for guests when we are busy.' So I hired him to help me entertain and pour for our guests on the patio overlooking the Napa River and throughout this beautiful property.

So, my plan was working and I was doing more outreach to drive in the business; so had to hire 2 more Wine Educators. Things were going just the way I had planned…

The Jackals had just come back from Maui and had met an artist whose paintings they really admired. They bought some of his very large pieces to fill the walls of our cavernous tasting room. "Wow! Those are gorgeous!" (not my style, but hey! Beauty is in the eye of the beholder, right?) They really filled the walls-how much could they have cost? I thought to myself. Couldn't have been cheap-and to ship from Hawaii? Yowch! But then I figured, well that seems to be his nouveau –riche style, what with his and hers matching Cadillac Escalades, and many other curious purchases for such a young, growing family with two businesses to run.

Where was the money coming from?

One day, I had just come back from visiting other wineries, dropping off collateral and other marketing materials when I heard from up the stairs:

"*Where's* my money?" shouted a voice I was not familiar with.

"Uh-oh. This can't be good", I said to myself. And as I tried to listen a little more, the voices in the room became muffled, then the door completely shut.

Minutes later, a little laughter seeped out of Jackal's office.

"Oh. Maybe not so bad after all." I quietly kept to myself. "Maybe that's just his sense of humor." So I went back to my office, and started fine tuning our first newsletter.

A couple of weeks went by and we carried on business as usual. One day, a very nice lady, a small vineyard grower, came in and said to me: "Hi. I met you before and I'm back to pick up the same check I was here to pick up 6 weeks ago for my grapes -is it ready?"

"Not sure", I replied pleasantly, let me go upstairs and see if our book keeper has it."

"Oh and I see you have added some nice new paintings and added other art since I was last here", she said matter of factly.

That made me feel a bit uncomfortable heading up to the accounting office, as I was pretty sure there was still no check. And I was right.

"No Maa'm. Sorry about that. I'll let him know you were here again."

"Would you please have Thomas call me? Thank you" she said politely and left.

About a week after that, two strapping young men in their late twenties from a very prominent vineyard management company came in to the tasting room.

"Thomas here?" one of them asked in a gruff and serious voice.

"No", I said. "He's outta town on business." They looked around the room like they meant business and didn't quite believe me.

"Really. He's not here. He's in Florida on business trying to get us a distributor there."

The two of them kept looking around the room, like Thomas might just come around the corner. I saw the look of determination in their eyes. They too were here to pick up a check or break his legs if he didn't pay up. Perhaps they just might smash those huge paintings and break anything else if they couldn't break his legs. I was very nervous-not for me-but for my staff of 3. Frankly, I couldn't blame them.

"Look, I know both of your parents and you have a very reputable company. Please don't do any harm to my staff or break anything. Let me go see if we have a check for you."

Just like before, there was no check. And there was no money in the bank for the book keeper to write one, anyway, she informed me.

I went back down stairs and apologized to the brothers. "When Thomas gets back, I'll have him call you."

One of the brothers responded "You know, all we have to do is call the ATF and they'll pull his license and shut you down!"

I nodded in understanding and off they went.

I went back up the stairs to speak with our book keeper.

"What do you mean there's no money in the bank?" I asked, somewhat in shock.

"Thomas always comes through, somehow." She tried to reassure me, slightly embarrassed to say it, even if not quite believing it herself. But, he always paid me.

I had heard something about some dealings with the Trefethens down in Oak Knoll, but never really knew what that was about. The next thing was a story that broke in the Napa newspaper, The Napa Valley Register, about a complaint from Constant Vineyards on Diamond Mountain. There was big brou-haha about these grapes that Constant sold to our winery. Our Viticulturist told me that she had seen the grapes with her very own eyes and they <u>were</u> sunburned and did not meet the specifications of the contract. She is an honest woman, so I believed her.

I saw and read the contract myself, it specifically spelled out the Brix range of acceptability. It was a very narrow margin. Maybe chalk this one up to Thomas.

I don't recall the exact day I met Dave Del Dotto at our tasting room, but he and Thomas had just completed a meeting. Thomas introduced me to Dave and said that they were business partners again and letting 'Bygones be bygones'. Dave and I shook hands and then I shook hands with Thomas congratulating him/them on their business venture. For some reason, I looked down at my right forearm after shaking hands with both men and felt odd. *(I just got a major shiver up my spine as I am writing and reliving this. REALLY!)*

Later that morning, I looked back at my forearm, and felt like there was some slimy 'ooze' seeping out of my pores on my forearm. I remember going home that night and telling my wife about this weird sensation and vibe from the handshake.

A couple of years later, after I was long gone from the Company, a very good friend of mine who is in the wine business forwarded me this e-mail he had received at his winery:

> *From: Desiree Del Dotto*
> *Date: Fri, Jul 31, 2015 at 3:09 PM*
> *Subject: Important Case that will affect Vintners in Napa Valley*
>
> *PLEASE TAKE A MOMENT AND READ THIS LETTER FROM MY DAD ABOUT OUR CRIMINAL CASE WITH OUR FORMER VINEYARD MANAGER. IF YOU FOLLOW US ON FACEBOOK HOPEFULLY YOU HAVE READ THIS AND SIGNED OUR PETITION. WE NEED YOUR HELP AND SUPPORT FOR JUSTICE. THANK YOU!*
>
> *Dear (Sir/Madam -ed.) -*
>
> *I have been growing grapes and making wine here in Napa Valley since 1990. You may have read that my former vineyard manager, ▮▮▮▮▮ ▮▮▮▮▮▮▮▮▮▮, LLC, was arrested for stealing grapes from my vineyards after harvests on both October 17 and October 21, 2014. On October 21, 2014 at 2:00 a.m., Mr. ▮ was caught stealing my Cabernet Sauvignon grapes from the harvest at our Oakville Vineyard as he diverted trucks to his own winery. We became aware of the theft that occurred on October 21st based upon information provided by Mr. ▮ employees. We were also informed that Mr. ▮ had previously stolen grapes from our Howell Mountain Vineyard on October 17th. While we were*

Audacious Scandalous Scoundrel

able to recover the grapes stolen on October 21st, we never recovered the grapes stolen on October 17th. The grapes that were stolen and not recovered were very valuable. With those grapes, we make wine that is sold for $195 a bottle. We lost grapes that would have produced 375 cases of wine thus resulting in a loss that exceeds $800,000.

As a result of the arrest, Mr. ▆ was charged with two felonies for grand theft. The criminal case against Mr. ▆ is known as the case of The People v. Jeffrey James Hill filed in Napa County Superior Court, Case No. ▆▆▆▆. Mr. ▆ arrest was chronicled in both the New York Times and the Napa Register.

On July 14, 2015, the District Attorney's Office entered into a plea agreement with Mr. ▆ wherein Mr. ▆ pled guilty to the theft that occurred on October 21st and, the charge for the theft on October 17th was dismissed. The sentencing hearing is scheduled for August 11, 2015 at 9:00 a.m. in Department E of the Napa County Superior Court located at 1111 3rd Street in Napa, California, Judge ▆▆▆▆▆▆▆ presiding. At the hearing, Mr. ▆ will ask that his felony conviction be reduced to a misdemeanor.

I intend to oppose any reduction of the crime from a felony to a misdemeanor. Upon request I can provide a copy of the letter that I submitted to the Court in support of a felony conviction including incarceration.

I believe that the investigation, prosecution and sentencing in this case affects every vintner in the wine business. Our businesses demand protection. One way that we obtain that protection is for potential criminals to know that the theft of grapes is a felony that results in incarceration. If Mr. ▆ is allowed to avoid jail time and only receive a misdemeanor conviction, then our County sets a precedent of minor punishment for what are major crimes against our businesses. Given the value of our grapes and our wine, potential criminals may decide to steal our grapes because the economic benefit of the crime outweighs the risk of the minor punishment that may result if caught. I do not want this message to be conveyed. Instead, I want the law to be a strong deterrent against such crimes so that potential criminals know that they will be convicted of a felony and sent to jail for stealing our grapes.

If you agree, I ask that you submit your opinion to the Court before the sentencing hearing on August 11 or by signing this online petition link.

Any letters of support can also be sent by email to ▓▓▓▓▓▓▓▓▓▓ at ▓▓▓▓▓▓▓▓▓▓▓▓▓▓▓▓ and addressed to The Honorable ▓▓▓▓▓▓▓▓▓▓▓▓▓, Napa County Superior Court, 1111 Third Street, Courtroom E, Napa, California 94559.

Sincerely,
Desiree Del Dotto on behalf of Dave Del Dotto
Del Dotto Vineyards

In June 2014, the Wine Company filed for bankruptcy in federal court, citing more than $8.6 million in debt. In August 2015, Jackal pled no contest and was sentenced to a year in jail by Napa County Superior Court for the 2013 theft of more than $50,000 worth of wine grapes from vineyards he was managing for another winery.

Appearing in federal court in Fresno on Wednesday, Jackal was charged with four counts of mail fraud and four counts of wire fraud. He faces a maximum penalty of 20 years in prison for each count plus possible fines.

TTB's 19 Charges:
1. Prior Felony Concealment
2. Lake County Cab Sold as Napa County Plus Forgery
3. Failure to Pay Taxes, Ever
4. Mislabeling of BevMo Cabernet Sauvignon
5. Attempted fraud
6. ASV North Coast Cabernet Sold As Napa Valley
7. Agajanian Sonoma Coast Chardonnay Sold As Napa Valley
8. Merlot Sold As Pinot Noir

9. Livermore Grapes Sold As Coombsville AVA
10. Changing Weigh Tags and AVA – Knightsen Contra Costa Vineyard
11. Wrap-it Transit Taxes Unpaid
12. Brand Sold, No Tax Paid
13. Manuscript Winery Taxes Kept
14. Whiskey River Ranch Winery
15. 300 Tons of Solano & Mendocino Cab Sold As Napa County to Lodi Buyers
16. Purple Pear and Affiant Get Solano Fruit Labeled as Napa Valley Cab
17. 50 tons of Lake County Merlot and Malbec Sold as Napa Valley Cab to Lodi Buyers
18. False Charitable Donation & Organic Claims
19. Lake County Truck Shipment Fraud

ASSHOLE!

"When we yell the loudest, we are really yelling at ourselves"-Sandrew

16

Defending Merlot - the "Sideways" effect

When the movie "Sideways" came out, it was only considered a "B" movie, but somehow it quickly became a cult classic, especially in the wine world. Most people don't know the whole story, so I'll give it to you, "straight up".

I got a call from the DTC Director of the Terlato Group (of the famous Tony Terlato family) to come in as business consultant and turn around Rutherford Hill Winery's tasting room. It had been hemorrhaging revenue for some time when the Direct –To-Consumer (DTC) as a whole was burgeoning. My charter was to come in boost morale, drive revenue and drive traffic. So, I wrote a business plan with 8 unique Experiences which would become streams of revenue that in turn, would drive traffic as well. It was up to me and my management style to turn around the morale of the tasting staff. They were a good team, just lacking direction and enthusiastic positive reinforcement.

I changed their position titles from "Tasting Room Assistants" to "Wine Educators" and trained them myself, elevating the caliber of experience they would deliver. I also re-wrote the Cave Tour script to make it much more relevant, salient and dynamic. If you've never been on cave tour, the outside is absolutely gorgeous, especially in the fall. These caves are the oldest for modern times and the longest in the Napa Valley.

Defending Merlot-the "Sideways" effect

Rutherford Hill Winery was originally called Souverain Rutherford, built by the late Joseph Phelps in 1973, for the Pilsbury Corporation. Yes, that's right, the one with the cute little dough boy on the commercials (Woo-hoooo!). After about 4 years, Pilsbury decided: 'You know what? We should stick to **baking!**'

So they sold the winery and caves to the Jaeger family who purchased it in 1977, changed the name to Rutherford Hill and made the first ever stand-alone Merlot. Merlot of course comes from Bordeaux, France where on the left bank of the Gironde River, it is a major blending grape due to its softer tannins. On the left bank, Cabernet Sauvignon is the dominant grape. Cabernet Sauvignon, of course is a hybrid of Cabernet Franc and Sauvignon Blanc. On the right bank, however, Merlot and Cabernet Franc are the dominant grapes, and Cabernet Sauvignon plays the supporting role. Merlot is often considered one of the "noble" grapes or grape of Nobility. I learned this when I was in the Guild of Master Sommeliers (btw, there were only 5 Master Somms at the time! Fred Dame and Evan Goldstein were my mentors) that there were 5 grapes of Nobility: Cabernet Sauvignon, Chardonnay, Pinot Noir, Syrah and Riesling. They're called the grapes of Nobility, because the Kings and Queens of Europe could obviously have whatever they wanted and these were the grapes for the wines they loved best. Some say besides Merlot, that Cabernet Franc and Sauvignon Blanc are noble grapes too.

In my days with California Wine Marketing, I had a small portfolio, but Merlot was *very* in vogue (after-all, we had gotten Americans to finally drop the "t" off " Mer lot"!). At that time the top four bestselling, most in demand "MER-los" were Shafer, Duckhorn, Keenan and Matanzas Creek and I represented all but Duckhorn. When I met Dan Duckhorn on his ranch, it was 117 degree day in July and he greeted us in Dungaree overalls with a six-pack of Miller beer! I didn't want to insult the man-no disrespect, but I sure as hell came here to taste the "Three Palms" Merlot-not beer.

Ok, so on with defending Merlot. Merlot was the flagship for Rutherford Hill; it's what built their reputation. Half of the production to this day is Merlot, and Tony Terlato, genius that he is, made it the huge success it is. He also pioneered the first ever wine shop in a grocery store in Chicago, was responsible for importing Santa Margherta Pinot Grigio to the states (still the number one selling Pinot Grigio) amongst *many* other accolades.

The Terlatos liked my business plan so much, they offered me the Tasting Room Manager position. And you know how it is when an Italian family makes you an offer, you can't refuse.

New "BORDEAUX MEETS NAPA" TASTING EXPERIENCE

Meet in our intimate cave setting for a seated tasting and explore how the classic Bordeaux varietals are expressed in our Napa Valley wines. Your wine-savvy guide will lead you through an interactive tasting experience featuring a collection of library and reserve tier bottlings from Rutherford Hill and Terlato Family Vineyards. Sip and savor the wines as you get a glimpse into New World and Old World wine history, the secrets of tasting like a professional and, of course, what makes Rutherford Hill so unique.

SUNDAYS, MONDAYS & THURSDAYS | 11:00 AM – 12:30 PM

$75 | $60 CLUB
Reservations required 48 hours in advance.

New TERLATO TERRACE

Enjoy the comfort of a table and ambiance of our patio as you sample a special flight of wines that include selections from both Rutherford Hill and our owners' namesake Terlato Family Vineyards label. Bring some friends or make new ones in this very festive atmosphere.

$30 | COMPLIMENTARY FOR CLUB MEMBERS

New Changes! OAK GROVE AL FRESCO TASTING

Bring your own gourmet lunch, gather around your linen-covered table in our serene Oak Grove and enjoy a selection of wines while you take in one of the best views of Napa Valley. With both our Premier and Luxury packages, you will receive a special three-bottle selection of our Napa Valley wines to explore and savor with your friends, as you gain insights and enjoy stories from a wine educator.

$100 PREMIER | $150 LUXURY
Table use complimentary for Club Members.
Reservations recommended.

"BLEND YOUR OWN MERLOT" EXPERIENCE

Be a winemaker for a day! After enjoying a wine tasting and tour of our popular caves, take a seat at your wine blending table. Guided by one of our wine educators, you will blend your own wine from a selection of our single vineyard Merlots and other varieties, bottle a half-bottle of your creation, and design your own unique wine label. Take your masterpiece home to share with friends and family!

SATURDAYS | 11:00 AM – 1:00 PM

$105 | $85 CLUB MEMBERS
Reservations required 48 hours in advance.

CAVE TASTING & TOUR

Take a tour of our nearly mile-long caves while sipping our delicious wines and learning about the Terlato family, our historic property and the winemaking process.

EVERY DAY | 11:30 AM, 1:30 PM & 3:30 PM
Reservations recommended.

TASTING FLIGHTS IN OUR TASTING ROOM

EVERY DAY
$20 CLASSIC FLIGHT | $30 SIGNATURE REDS
No reservations required.

For information and to book an experience, call (707) 963-1871 ext. 2249 or visit www.rutherfordhill.com
For private experiences for 14 guests or more, please contact our Events Dept. at ext. 2218.

200 RUTHERFORD HILL ROAD, RUTHERFORD, CA 94573

The new programs for RHW from my business plan

Defending Merlot-the "Sideways" effect

The "Bordeaux meets Napa" experience was my show that I had developed over the years starting with that first Wine Maker Dinner for Mayacamas at Elarios, only this time with Rutherford Hill wines. The pinnacle was partnering with Executive Chef Curry from Auberge du Soleil, the five star resort and restaurant. Here's a sample menu we performed:

Maddalena Party						Sunday, November 9, 2014

Executive Chef Curry, Auberge du Soleil, Sandrew Montgomery, Sommelier

First Course

Day Boat Scallops, Prosciutto, Cauliflower, Lemon, Golden Raisin Vinaigrette

Rutherford Hill Sauvignon Blanc "Napa Valley" 2013

Second Course

Kona Kampachi Crudo, Sesame Crème Fraîche, Cucumber, Radish, Dashi

Terlato Family Vineyards Pinot Grigio "Russian River" 2011

Third Course

Sonoma Chicken, Glazed Chestnuts, Cipollini, Verjus Poached Quince

Rutherford Hill Limited Release Chardonnay "Los Carneros" 2012

Fourth Course

Northern Halibut, Brussel Sprouts, Chorizo, Manila Clams, Parsley Jus

Rutherford Hill Rose' of Merlot "Napa Valley" 2013 "Saignee"

Even though <u>Sideways</u> had been out for over 10 years, the impact from the infamous line was still taking a toll on Merlot sales and wine enthusiasts just could not shake it off. Their minds were made up: 'I am *not* a Merlot drinker!' The impact created a devastating effect on the wine industry, but it ended up being a good thing-and I'll explain why.

If you have not seen the movie (yet!), it's a "buddy movie" about 2 Southern California men on a Boys Weekend (you girls can't have all the fun!) for a final 'hurrah' before "Jack" (played by Thomas Hayden Church) gets married. His Best Man, "Miles" (played by Paul Giamatti) has plans for a weekend of golf and wine tasting in Santa Barbara County. Harmless, until it all goes sideways....

Miles' character establishes himself early on as a wine expert and snob, teaching his college friend about wine tasting, etiquette ("Gum?! Are you chewing gum?!") and wine appreciation ("and just a soussant of asparagus", whatever that means). When they arrive at the Los Olivos Café, Miles utters the infamous line to Jack: "If they're drinking Merlot, I'm NOT DRINKING any *FUCKIN'* Merlot!!"

Wow! Holy sheesh! Miles is the supposed 'expert' and apparently it's no longer cool to drink Merlot.

Most of the audience never recalls why he makes that infamous statement because he says it so adamantly. It was because his EX-wife loved Merlot, in the movie. In the *movie*. In the book, it was Cabernet Sauvignon that she loved so much, but Paul Giamatti could not pronounce "Sauvignon", so Director Alexander Payne took the liberty to change the script to Merlot, not realizing that in real life it would have such a *huge* impact on Merlot sales. And they plummeted, almost instantly. Why I say that that was a good thing is that Merlot grapes were in such demand at the time, many growers were being greedy and getting away with not thinning the crop halfway through the growing season. That's what you have to do to produce high quality grapes/wine. When you drop half the crop of grape clusters, it doubles up the energy into the remaining clusters, making high quality fruit. So, if you stayed in the Merlot game, you had to thin the crop and that's the good news for the consumer. High quality Merlots are back in the market and the best producers always thinned the crop, anyway. I had to defend this on a daily basis while at Rutherford Hill.

Now for the rest of the story...

In the course of the movie, Miles also ironically retorts a couple of times that he does not care for Cabernet Franc as well. Throughout Sideways, Miles makes references to his favorite special bottle that he has been saving for 'that special'

Defending Merlot-the "Sideways" effect

occasion (hoping it would be in celebration of his novel getting published-I get that!). Being the loser he is, we find him in a fast food joint, drinking this special occasion wine out of a Styrofoam cup (of all things!) the highly prized 1961 Cheval Blanc, which comes from 'the right bank'; comprised of Cabernet Franc and Merlot!

I noticed I was the only one in the theater laughing that day.

I may have mentioned that Kat's family is from San Luis Opisbo, so because of our own love of Pinot Noir, we would often find ourselves in the tasting rooms in Santa Barbara in Lompoc, "The Grotto" and downtown in the "Ghetto". Of course we *just had to* dine in the Los Olivos Café where Miles goes to the 'Dark Side' and utters that vicious and demeaning statement. We also just had to dine at The Hitching Post restaurant where we shared our Bottle Shock story with Chef Owner Frank Ostintini who shared with us his 'hand cameo' where he sticks his hands through the kitchen pass through window. That night we were seated at the table right where the cameraman must have been training the camera on Jack and Miles at the bar. As we were enjoying our dinner, 3 couples swiftly entered the front door (which was visible from our table) and without hesitation proceeded to stand right by us staring at the bar. It was quite apparent that they had been out wine tasting all day.

In their eyes you could just see that they were imagining-no, they actually *could* see Jack and Miles sitting at the bar-almost as if they wanted to approach them-but suddenly, they became self-concious, turned back to look at Kat and me, realizing they were intruding on our dinner and space and with that, Poof! They ran right back out the door!

Another time we were in this area meeting friends and the rendezvous point was conveniently Pea Soup Andersens. Behind this restaurant is the Tourism Bureau. So we popped in and discovered they had several maps of the area and other touristy things to do. I noticed this one particular lime green map. "Is that a map of were 'Sideways' was filmed?" I inquired. "Yes." Said the lady behind the counter. As she reached to pull it off the rack and hand it to me, she added rather vehemently, "We want you to know we do NOT have large grown men running around here in Santa Barbara County!" Kat and I laughed really hard. But she was *serious*, and started to put the map back as she apparently thought we were disrespecting her comment, but of course we thought she was joking. "Lady. It's just a movie." I thought, but instead I said "Oh, OK." She reluctantly handed me the map and we were on our way.

17

The Napa Valley Jazz Getaway

    I met the great Smooth Jazz musician extraordinaire Brian Culbertson while I was managing Rutherford Hill. I was already a big fan of his and the local jazz station KJZY had been promoting the hell out of the show. On the radio's website they were running video clips of Culbertson with one of my all-time heroes, the incomparable Maurice White, Sheldon, also of Earth, Wind and Fire,

The Napa Valley Jazz Getaway

as well as Dave Koz, and Ray Parker, Jr. for the upcoming show at Rodney Strong Vineyards in Healdsburg. I couldn't stand it anymore-I just *had* to go. What an exhilarating show!

My counterpart Richard at sister winery Chimney Rock, had asked me if I was into jazz and had I ever heard of Brian Culbertson. I told him I am and I had and I'm a huge fan, so he said, "Well, I hosted him and we had Ray Parker Jr. play a special, intimate performance at the Winery in the barrel room for the Napa Valley Jazz Getaway VIPs last year."

"Cool!" I responded enthusiastically." If you do that again, please let me know, I'd love to come."

"Well that's just it." Richard went on to say. "Brian doesn't like to do the same venue twice-trying to spread the love. That's why I think you should give Kim Zimmer a call and invite them to RHW. I'll e-mail you her contact info-she's the one who puts the whole schedule together and she's great to work with".

Man, was I excited!

So I contacted Kim and she said that she, Brian, David, Kyle and Luke would be coming out in February researching venues and would be interested in checking us out. *Hot Damn!*

February rolled around and I hosted the whole Napa Valley Jazz Getaway team on property showing them different areas where potentially he could play and we could entertain the VIP's for lunch on the Friday of this 5 day event.

Brian told me, "I have this concept I've been working on: 'P2P'; Piano to Piano with David Benoit and myself-I may even want to play my trombone!" "David Benoit", I thought to myself, "All-RIGHTY then!"

Realizing that the RHW property was being interviewed for the possibility of such a one of a kind experience, I wanted to make sure we put our best foot forward for that first impression, so I poured everybody a glass of the Reserve Merlot (Miles be damned!) and took us all out to the picnic grounds overlooking the '50 yard line' of the Napa Valley.

As we got to the most optimal spot, I turned to Brian and asked, "Can you see yourself and David performing right here?!" His response was immediate: "Yes! Yes I can."

Knowing that Brian had covered and recorded Earth, Wind and Fire's "Serpentine Fire", Kool and The Gang's "Hollywood Swingin" and influenced by so many other Funk bands, I told Brian, "I'm a funky white boy too! And have been inspired by so many of the same artists as you. In fact, a few years ago in

San Francisco George Clinton and Bootsy Collins came to town as P-Funk and I could *not* miss that. When I first got up on the speakers to dance, they both looked at me, like 'you should not be up there, crazy white boy' and then they saw me dance and looked at each other, as if to say 'hmmm, he's ok, let him be'. And then Clinton looked over at the roadies who were coming my way and said on the mic, approvingly, "He can dance. Let him dance!"

Brian nodded his head in acknowledgement and said, "Yeah! Think I'll bring my trombone too."

I showed the NVJG team other potential spots on the property, but Brian came back and said

"No! We're gonna do P2P on the first spot you showed us". We shook hands and made it a deal.

The event wasn't until June, so I had time to think about how I wanted to introduce him and Benoit, as I was going to be the M.C. I had over 3 months to script it out. I pretty much knew how I wanted to start the show, but I wasn't quite sure if it would be pc.

I stewed on this for about the entire 3 months. So I asked Kim about a week before the show and told her exactly what I had in mind. Her response? "Uh, yeah... (In that kind of 'yea-No!' tone) Let me ask Brian and I'll get back to you". Well, she never did.

So, on the morning of the show, while David and Brian were with me in our VIP room and chatting, I turned to Brian and said "So here's how I'd like to introduce you two..."

As many nights as I practiced this in my head for nearly 3 months, there it was. I just laid it out right then and there. Brian's reaction? He didn't say a thing. He just leaned over the table towards me looking over the top of his sunglasses with his trademark spiky blond hair and gave me a *look*.

But I wasn't quite sure if he was expressing "What do <u>you</u> think!" or " You realize that well over half my audience is African American, right?" or "WTF?!".

We had some good laughs, talked story, I reviewed the set list for the show and Benoit and Culbertson signed in gold pen about 30 wine bottles of all kinds to be sold after the P2P show, including Rutherford Hill's flagship Bordeaux blend "Episode".

Now it was show time and time for us to walk over to those 2 shiny, beautiful Grand Pianos, side by side on this classic, gorgeous Northern California day. There was Brian's silver trombone laying on the stage, as well. This was a private concert for all 56 NVJG's VIPs and they were all assembled awaiting our arrival. I looked over the crowd and assessed the audience. I grabbed the microphone and proceeded.

"Hello everybody and welcome to the Napa Valley! We're on the 50 yard line of the Napa Valley just to give you an idea of where you are geographically. A couple of weeks ago I was listening to the Dave Koz Lounge on Sirus XM and he was promoting this very event, and he said it was 'quite the Hang!' So I ask you Ladies and Gentlemen, is this quite the Hang?!"

The adoring crowd gave a very warm response of gratefulness and approval.

"And now Ladies and Gentlemen, it is my great honor and privilege to present to you, two of the greatest jazz artists and composers of our time. First, the man who brought back Charles Schultz' Peanuts and Charlie Brown with 'Linus and Lucy', Mr. Da-vid Benoit!" I waited for the audience's applause to die down. "And now, the Master Mind of the Napa Valley Jazz Getaway, the Funky White Boy himself, BRI-AN CulbertSAAAAAAN!!"

The crowd went *nuts*! Ah! There. I said it! Finally after all those nights for 3 months, waking up in the middle of the night rehearsing it in my head and then thinking to myself, you will never be invited to another BC show. But the audience *loved* it!

That night, at the Friday Night Funk Fest at the Lincoln Theater, Brian and his band played the song "Play That Funky Music White Boy". Man, am I glad I said it after all. Could you imagine how bummed I would have been had I *not* introduced him like that?

Dancing Somm

After the show, I took a selfie (which was very new at the time-Ellen Degeneres had not yet taken that famous selfie where she was the host of the Oscars, which then made "selfies" blow up!) with David Benoit. I was telling him about the Red Baron airplane that Charles Schultz, a resident of Sonoma County, used in his Peanuts comic strip to fight Snoopy. The Red Baron resides at the Sonoma County Airport, and rarely if ever flew over to the Napa side of the Mayacamas Mountains. But *it did* <u>that</u> day! 10 minutes before David played 'Linus and Lucy', it circled overhead at our concert. And that's what I'm saying to him as we take this selfie. A year later, Benoit has a new song out, called "The Red Baron".

The Napa Valley Jazz Getaway

I feel so honored to call Brian my friend. He has literally introduced me to several of today's great contemporary jazz artists: Michael Lington, Marion Meadows, Eric Marienthal, Eric Darius, Marquel Jordon, Candy Dulfer, Vincent Ingala, Straight No Chaser, Huge Groove, Gerald Albright, Keiko Matsui, Jonathan Butler and Peter White.

Peter and I look somewhat alike. At the 2017 Napa Valley Jazz Getaway, as I was dancing off to the side of the stage to Pieces of a Dream, after White's set, a black man came up to me and asked me if I was Peter White. "I'm white, but I'm not *that* White!" I responded with a triple entendre. We both laughed. He shook my hand and went back into the crowd and I went back to dancing. The next year at the NVJG, I saw Peter after his set signing CDs. I went up to him and said, "All these people keep coming up to me and wanting me to sign *your* CDs-maybe we should take a pic together and dispel the myth." He laughed and obliged.

When the next set started, I was back in that exact same spot dancing off stage right where the previous year I had been mistaken for Peter. And then Mr. White came within 10 feet of me, enjoying Bobby Caldwell and I leaned over to Peter "Thanks for your new album and bringing back great classics like 'Groovin', "Do I do', 'Sittin' on the Dock of the Bay' and 'Heard It through the Grapevine", I said. "Glad you enjoy them. Some of my favorites growing up in England. We like that Motown stuff, too!"

It was Brian who I first texted when Prince died and as well as when Maurice White died, being that we are kindred spirits in soul and funk.

Soon after I came to work at Joseph Phelps Vineyards, Ray Parker Jr. was a guest tasting the JPV wines with friends. I knew he was on the reservation books and hoped to meet him. On their way out, I turned to Ray and said "You and I have a mutual friend." "Oh yeah. Who's that?" Ray Jr. asked. "Brian Culbertson," I replied. "Oh Really? Culbertson? Get over here and let's take a selfie and I'll send it to him!"

He grabbed me by the shoulder-*he's a lot bigger dude than I realized*-and spun me around in the foyer of the retail room. click, swoosh. "There. Just sent it to Brian. What's your name?" as he stuck out his hand. "Sandrew. Sandrew Montgomery." "How d' you know Culbertson?" Parker asked.

So I told him of my involvement with the Napa Valley Jazz Getaway. "Oh. That's cool! Maybe I'll see you next year! It was *so* nice to meet you."

The Napa Valley Jazz Getaway

"The pleasure was all mine. Thanks for the selfie!"

About a year later at JPV, I was hosting four ladies from Tennessee. It was ladies' weekend and they were out having a ball. I poured them the wines and entertained their questions. As we were making the connection, I asked them if they were into smooth jazz, contemporary jazz.

"Oh yeah! Absolutely." The ladies responded.

"Have you ever heard of Brian Culbertson's Napa Valley Jazz Getaway?"

"No."

"How about David Benoit?"

"That sounds familiar."

"Well, every second week of June –it's a 5 daylong event, Brian brings great acts to the Napa Valley-of course including his own funk band. In the past, on Saturdays and Sundays they've had Chaka Kahn, The Temptations, Michael McDonald, Bony James, Gerald Albright, Spyro Gyra-you name it! Friday night's the FUNK night with the Ohio Players, The Family Stone, with Larry Graham (but without Sly). On Thursday nights, it's more of the traditional jazz artists such as Al Jareau, Earl Klugh, David Benoit and Four Play."

"Oh I love Four Play!" one of the ladies exclaimed. To which her friends broke out into hysteria. When the laughter finally subsided, her friend next to her said,

"Honey. We *ALL* love foreplay!"

18

"Terroir", "Tannin", "Flavor Profile", "Balance" – Explained

These are terms and concepts that are bandied about in tasting rooms, but rarely-if ever-explained. I ask guests all the time: "Are you familiar with these?"

Nods all abound. "But do you *really* know what they are or mean?"

Heads invariably shake "no". These are <u>essential</u> pieces of the conundrum of wine speak that need addressing, not glossing over.

Flavor Profile

So much of this tome *is* about the "Flavor Profile". It is the crux of how I come up with my signature recipes and pairings, by breaking down the flavor profile of the wine first. Please see the chapter where I break down into spectrums and demystify the flavor profile. The flavor profile is derived by the sun's warmth that drives the sugars and constitutes the "flesh" of the wine. The yang to that is the acidity that creates the structure, therefore the "backbone" to the wine. Acidity is derived from the cooling or Maritime influences. In Sonoma, the Maritime influences are the Pacific Ocean, the Russian River and the fog. On the Napa side, they are the San Pablo Bay (northern part of San Francisco Bay), the Napa River and of course, the fog. That's why the Mediterranean climate of Napa and Sonoma is ideally suited for wine grape growing. According to the Napa Valley Vintners and Growers Association, only 2 % of the world enjoys this type of climate.

Terroir

So what exactly is "terroir"? Many think it's a bullshit French marketing term or just the soil-it's more than that. Its *many* things that are climate driven, thus the winemaker's quest for the Holy Grail to make wine with "a sense of place". It includes the soils, microclimates, the amount of sunshine or the lack thereof, the amount of rain or lack thereof, maritime influences, as well as accent or positioning.

"Terroir", "Tannin", "Flavor Profile", "Balance" – Explained

Maritime influences include oceans, rivers, lakes and bays. It also includes the fog and wind-what I refer to as the "pre-cursor fog wind", which precedes the fog as the initial wisps turn into layers. Take a look at maps of the great and soon to be discovered great wine regions of the world and you will find this to be true. That is why, where I live and work in Napa and Sonoma are World-Class growing regions. Specifically in Napa, you have to the south, the northern part of the greater San Francisco Bay, the San Pablo Bay which is fed by the Napa River. The Napa River flows through the entire Napa Valley, connecting from the confluence of creeks and other tributaries beginning in Calistoga, to the north. This is where Mount St. Helena is; a volcano that blew over one and half million years ago, depositing over 100 different soil types in the 32 mile stretch we call the Napa Valley. It is the only place on Earth to boast having 50% of ALL the world's soil types. That's a huge part of what makes the Napa Valley so unique and special, as do the micro climates and the Mountain Ranges that form the Valley. One day during the growing season, I was leaving Domaine Carneros where I used to be a manager and drove up valley to Calistoga. Every mile I drove got a degree warmer on my car's thermostat. It went from 72 degrees Fahrenheit to 113!

On the Sonoma side, you have the maritime influences of the Pacific Ocean and the Russian River in addition to fog and wind. That's why the thin skinned grapes Pinot Noir and Chardonnay from the cool Burgundy region, thrive here. It also has a unique soil type, Goldridge Sandstone, only found in one spot on the planet, western Sonoma County. It is a fusion of sand and fossils. So porous, it is idyllic for drainage, creating tiny berries, rich in concentration that create layers of unctuousness.

Most winery folks don't talk about the wind much. But it is very influential as a key ingredient of **balance**, as the first 2 key components of *balance* begins right in the vineyards with 1) the acids and 2) the fruit sugars. Later in the day and evenings when the precursor fog wind rolls in, it blows up the skirt of the vine's canopy opening it up and exposing the grapes to the sun's warmth therefore developing the sugar in the berries that will ultimately become the flavor profile of the wine. Once the fog settles in, it's cooling the grapes down and in turn increasing the acidity levels. And of course the next morning, the sun beats down, burning off the fog and warming up the berries for a nice even-keeled balance between the acid levels and fruit sugars on a daily basis.

"Accent" is what vintners and vineyard managers refer to as the way the vines are situated and direction they are facing, so as to maximize optimal growing conditions predicated on the respective grape varietal and the circumstances which they are best suited to develop. For instance, we have learned through trial and error that Zinfandel sunburns easily and is subject to premature raisining. Thus, in the Northern Hemisphere, it is best to plant rows on hills that are northeast facing. This is because while the sun is rising from the east in the morning, the grapes will still most likely be submerged in the fog or at least still cool form the evening's 45-55 degree temps and will be shadowed by the hill in the hottest part of the day. In California, this can often be between 3:00 pm to 6:00 pm. There is a saying: 11 to 11. The fog rolls in around 11:00 at night and pulls back around 11:00 in the morning. Whereas the thick skin Bordeaux varietals (Cabernet Sauvignon, Cabernet Franc, Peteit Verdot, Malbec and Merlot) can not only take the intense heat but flourish in that same period in the afternoon.

Balance

So we have the first two components of balance, the acids and the sugars, now on to the other four. 3) Ph is very important from a chemistry perspective and all I will say is that it needs to be 3.0 or 3.5 on the scale of alkalinity. *The intent of this book is to entertain you-not have your eyes glaze over!*

On to 4)

Tannins. Most everybody who enjoys wine has heard of tannins because we in the biz talk about them-but does anybody ever *really* tell you what they are? Most folks feel like they would be "found out" to be stupid if they asked, so they don't. Rest assured, there *are* no dumb questions! I'm still a student after 40 years and I've even taught at the Napa Valley College-*really interesting* topics like "Clones" and "Biodynamic Farming". <u>*If you're ever having a tough time getting to sleep at night, just Google those topics!*</u>

Ok, so first of all, tannins are the natural preservative that allows the wine to lay down in the cellar and *hopefully* improve with time and all aspects become fully integrated. Tannins are also the thing that turns your mouth into a fish, and the most challenging aspect to wine and food pairings.

From a physiological standpoint, as the wine enters your mouth, the tannins immediately seek out the proteins in your saliva and glom on to them, thereby sucking in your cheeks and thus the fish effect phenomenon. It's what the French call '*sauvage*' ("So Vaj"), savage-the <u>attack of the palate</u>.

Do you remember the first time somebody handed you a glass of red wine and said: "Here. Try this-it's *really great*-it's *really* expensive and you're gonna love

"Terroir", "Tannin", "Flavor Profile", "Balance" –Explained

it!"? Most people's response is something akin to "Can I be honest with you? Not so much!"

So where do tannins come from? There are four places: 1) skins 2) seeds 3) stems and 4) the oak barrels have wood tannins. When I conduct a component tasting, I will have people taste a tea bag and put it on the tip of their tongue. It's the same as peeling back the skin of a grape and tasting the inside has the same effect, the bitter astringency. We all have the same reaction: recoiling with a squinched up face. The physical equivalent of "Ewwwww"!

I mentioned the wood tannins. We want the 5) oak to be in balance too- meaning how new the barrel is, how much time the wine has aged in the barrel and also factoring in if the wine was fermented in the barrel. Wine makers should be concerned with the over use of a brand new barrel-it all depends if that particular varietal can handle it and stand up too all that overpowering influence. Come see me sometime and we can geek out more about oak.

Have you guessed number six yet?

That's ok. Most people don't get it right, perhaps because subliminally *they don't want to. It's alcohol. That's' right, alcohol.* When I first started selling wine when the dinosaurs roamed, all wines were 12.5 % alcohol across the board. Didn't matter whether it was a blend or 100% varietal. *And there was no discussion of "new world" vs. "old world".*

What changed? Two things.

The Millennial Generation wanted more bang for their buck for one. Secondly, a particular wine writer whose influence dominated the viniferous landscape.

So there was a trend toward higher alcohol. How winemakers arrive at 12.5% alcohol is by picking the grapes at 25 degrees brix. That's the sugar level and the formula works roughly by cutting that in half. California grapes were being picked at 30, 32 and even 34 degrees brix. Now cut that in half. Here's what you need to know: once you get to 18 % alcohol, you are in a whole new tax bracket. Nobody wants to pay those tariffs, right? 'Cause the winery will have to raise the price and pass that on to you. So! You get a 1% "fudge factor" over 14.5 %-so everybody knocks that number back down. Now don't get me wrong. I'm all for a party!

My point is, if you want to show off your signature dishes, you don't want to compete with the alcohol-BUT! If you're a lousy chef, by all means, go right on a head.

19

Jess Jackson, Maverick; Matanzas Lavender

The first time I met Jack Davies of Schramsberg was in 1985 in Denver Colorado at the headquarters for the distributer, Western –Davis. I mentioned to Jack the challenges of selling his ultra- premium sparkling wine in competition with French Champagne. I asked if it would be possible to discount the wine so we could get broader distribution and sell it by the glass. His quick response: "Young man, if you believe in your product, never, EVER discount it!" A lesson I have taken to heart in all my business endeavors and why I consider him a great mentor.

This is also where I met Jess Jackson. It was just Jess with his winemaker Jed Steele. That's really all there was at the time to what would eventually become the "KJ Empire", an International "Tour de Force" on the global wine market. They were here that day to introduce a brand new wine called Kendall Jackson's "Vintners Reserve" Chardonnay. Who knew that we would make it America's bestselling Chardonnay by the glass of all time!

It was exactly what America needed at that time. Chardonnay was after all a noble grape, it had a hint of sweetness for the American palate, they could pronounce it and were drinking more white than red wine at that time, plus restaurants and their patrons were becoming very comfortable with paying for premium wine by the glass-in fact, it was quite de rigger!

After I left Colorado and moved to San Diego, I was part of the California Wine Marketing Brokerage. Part of our tiny portfolio was Matanzas Creek Winery owned by Bill and Sandra McKeiver. Sandra was Heiress to the Sears Roebuck fortune and took her money to create Matanzas Creek winery, nestled in the hills of Bennett Valley in southern central Sonoma County. (The original winemaker was Merry Edwards, the "Queen of Pinot" who I would work with in years to come; her successor was David Ramey. Quite a pedigree!)

Jess Jackson, Maverick; Matanzas Lavender

It was Sandra, who was so inspired by the Lavender growing in Provence, France, that she planted incredible gardens encompassing the grounds of the very remote winery. For decades cultures and artists from all around the world have come to paint and photograph these beautiful little purple gems that blossom both in June and then again in August-quite a spectacular beauty!

(I love grilling plump, juicy, bone –in chicken breasts with the skin on. When you flip the breasts over to skin side down, sprinkle Lavender flowers directly on the charcoals. The soapy perfume of the flowers, when cooked, gives the skin a cinnamon scent that is absolutely delicioso!)

Sandra and Bill asked me out for dinner one evening in 1987 to discuss the future of Matanzas Creek.

We had a wonderful dinner and I asked them if they had ever thought of selling the winery. Sandra laughed and said firmly "No." And then added quickly, "Unless somebody offered me 5 million!" She and Bill laughed again. I was excited about the future and what role I might play. Before we could finalize plans, the McKeivers had another dinner out, at the request of Jess Jackson.

As the story goes, Jess greeted them and asked them to join him pointing to 2 vacant chairs at the table.

As the McKeivers sat down, Jess turned and said," I'm sure you know why I invited you here tonight." Sandra said simply and matter of factly, "The winery's not for sale." Jess looked a bit puzzled at Sandra first and then Bill.

He then grabbed his cocktail napkin, pulled a pen out of his sport coat pocket and scribbled just 3 characters down: 45 M and passed the napkin over to Sandra, but so that Bill could see. They gave a quick, knowing glance to each other.

"Sold!" she exclaimed.

Jess's response? "Waiter! Your <u>best</u> Champagne, please!"

Guess the journey for the Napa and Sonoma Wine Sherpa was not climbing up *that* mountain, after all.

The next time I saw Jess he was at John Ash and Company restaurant in Santa Rosa where I was treating my wife to lunch on her birthday, where we were seated at the next table to Mr. Jackson. I introduced Kat to Jess and said, "By the way, Kat works for you at Matanzas Creek." Ever the Gentleman, he stood up with his imposing stature, shook her hand and said, "Oh, that's great! Always nice to meet a fellow co-worker. Happy Birthday!" And that was it for years to come.

The next 2 times I saw Jess were at funerals, unfortunately. Ironically, they were 3 months a part. The founding owners of Alexander Valley Vineyards (also part of California Wine Marketing's portfolio), Harry and Maggie Wetzel were up in years; Harry went first. It was an absolutely stunning day with the services being held at the Wetzel home in Healdsburg. Many, many Sonoma wine dignitaries were there paying their respects to one of this region's wine pioneers.

There were many great stories of Harry and Maggie, memories and reminiscing and polite laughter. Jess Jackson spoke eloquently to the gathering about having first set foot on the Wetzel property. While waiting for Harry to show up to discuss business, Maggie greeted him and immediately had him get down on his hands and knees to help her plant some artichokes and other vegetables in "Maggie's Garden". He was reluctant to do so in his business attire. But! After all, it was the famed Maggie's Garden. (For decades AVV has been making a wine called 'Maggie's Farm' in homage to the Matron.)

You could tell by all the laughter, that several in attendance had been commanded to do the same thing in the first encounter with Maggie.

I was now very good friends with the youngest Wetzel, John, who married one of my very best and dearest friends, Lauren Lockwood, who I have known since we met the first week of my freshman year at the University of Denver. Of course I had worked with his sister Katie and brother Hank in selling their brand in San Diego.

Jess and I spoke and he reminded me that just like Robert Mondavi, he started his own winery at age 52. That got me to thinkin', I ain't even fifty yet. Maybe it's not too late to start mine after all?!

Three months later, Maggie Wetzel had passed. It was a déjà vu day. Equally as stunning a beautiful day as Harry's celebration of life, held at the same location and pretty much all the same people showing their respects, as we had all done with Harry.

The Reverend presiding was also the same as Harry's. He quipped that "Harry and Maggie tried a trial separation -apparently that didn't work out!"

As before, Jess Jackson and I struck up a conversation. He turned to me and said, "You know, Sandrew, I have just been to 6 countries in 2 weeks!"

"Why are you doing that to yourself, Jess? After all, you own 32 International Wineries…" He promptly corrected me, "36!"

"Ok, all the *more* reason; why are you doing that to yourself?"

"I'm afraid if the bus stops, what might happen."

(I had no idea he had been diagnosed with cancer.)

The day the Santa Rosa Press Democrat newspaper's front page had this picture of Jess in the vineyards, I didn't have to read the headlines, I knew the bus had stopped.

20

Carneros and the Chateau on the Plateau

Los Carneros is the only AVA or American Viticulturally Area to straddle both Napa and Sonoma. Close to the northern part of the San Francisco Bay called the San Pablo Bay, the Carneros region is ideally suited for the thin skinned grapes of Burgundy, Chardonnay and Pinot Noir, especially well-suited to making sparkling wine. In the youthful part of my career, I helped market this region as *the* premier area for Pinot and Chard. This was pre power point, so my presentation was using my left fist balled up to represent San Francisco. I would take my right hand over my middle knuckles and point and say "You go over the Golden Gate Bridge about an hour away from the City and the fog rolls in here –perfect for these 2 Burgundian Varietals…" It was pretty ridiculous looking back now, but hey necessity is the mother of invention, right?!

When I lived in San Diego, I regularly received Wine Spectator magazine and one issue, the cover was of this exquisite French Chateau. It was fabulous! Now the architectural landscape was just beginning to change for wineries, but this? Oh, man! This was truly a magnificent thing of beauty, Domaine Carneros. I would come to affectionately call it "The Chateau on the Plateau". I knew when I saw that magazine cover, the next time I visited the Napa Valley that would be my first stop.

The impressive Domaine Carneros, home of Le Reve

Carneros and the Chateau on the Plateau

On May 22, 1994, Kat and I had our third date on the corner table here on the far right. It was magical and the most appropriate place for a third date, ifin' ya knowhattamean (and I think ya do!) The bubbles were flowing, the view gorgeous (and so was Kat!), the conversation, fantastic-now this, this *is* the life!

My Dad came to visit us for Thanksgiving one year and even though he wasn't a wine drinker, I knew he'd enjoy this view and the Chateau. (He just wanted to go to the A & W in St. Helena for a chocolate shake!) The very last picture I ever took with my Dad was taken half way up this staircase.

This was Claude Tattinger's dream (Le Reve) to replicate his family's 17th century chateau here in California. He came to Napa, to start Tattinger Champagne's American counterpart and "to find his man to run it". He made it well known, he was here to find his man to be in charge, as he would spend most of his time in Champagne. Several people in the know, suggested Monsieur Tattinger should meet with Eileen Crane during his Executive Search process. Apparently, as the story goes, he seemed a bit agitated with this as he was on a mission to find his *man* to oversee operations for his new venture. Eventually the stoic and resolutely French gentleman acquiesced and met with the very accomplished Ms. Crane. On the third round of interviews, Eileen turned to Claude and very matter of factly stated: "Do I have the job, or not?" Apparently that was man enough for him, as Eileen has been the Chief Winemaker and CEO of the operation from the beginning and continues on as of this writing. She is an amazing and gifted person, as those are two *entirely different* skill sets and she has been performing them extremely well for over twenty-five years!

Cheers!

I was thrilled when I got the call to come interview for a manger position at Domaine Carneros. I was hired there to manage in the Chateau as well as the Wine Club. Eileen knows I love music (and probably that I love to dance) and asked me to be a part of the reviewing committee for an innovative concept: Can music *enhance* the wine tasting experience? The idea was wine pairing with a completely different approach. After all they're both art, so it makes sense, right? It was quite an experiment. We tried various glasses of our sparklers with four kinds of music. Classical, contemporary, modern jazz and an oldie but goody from the 60's. The most classic combination, naturally, was the classical music paired with Le Reve. And to some extent it worked. The up and down tempos and the crescendo was distracting though and took away from the mood when the piece was not in between tempos and consistently flowing in an even keeled manner. As you know I love jazz, but it too was distracting, as I was enjoying the music and not paying attention to the bubbles. The "oldie but goody" was even more so, as I tried to sing along (and remember) with the lyrics in my head. The contemporary song was one I was not all the familiar with, so I tried to pay attention and understand the lyrics, the rhythm and to become familiar with it, so it was actually taking away from these phenomenal sparkling wines. Interesting concept, but the majority take away was this did not work. Maybe we didn't have the right songs or even genres; or maybe, I'm just too into music!

When the Golden State Warriors basketball team started their dynasty run, the whole Bay Area was a buzz with how good they really are-even before Kevin Durant. The "Splash Brothers", Steph Curry and Klay Thompson were very impressive and just *so* fun to watch. Now I admit I got on the band wagon a little late, but they made the game so exciting, it felt like the Michael Jordon, Scottie Pippin days of the Chicago Bulls.

The day that Steph's parents, Sondra and Dell (a NBA great himself) came to Domaine Carneros, my staff was so excited. Naturally they asked me if they could go up and ask them to take pictures with them. "I understand. I'd like to too, but we gotta leave 'em alone and let them enjoy themselves quietly." "Aww, comeon, man!" "Seriously, NO!"

Of course one of the great things about being a manager is that *I* could go up and speak to them. "How is your experience with us today, folks?"

"Very nice. Very nice. Such a beautiful place" Sonya replied.

"And the bubbles?" I asked with a shiteatin' grin.

"Fantastic!" Dell was quick to respond.

"As you know, we are <u>all</u> proud of your son. It's sucha joy to watch him play- *so fun!*"

"We don't understand what all the fuss is about-*we* are getting *so* much attention! We're just his parents."

"Well, a toast to Steph and the Dub Nation. Thanks for joining us today. Go Warriors!" I said as I shook their hands and parted to leave them to enjoy their peace.

21

Visualize Whirrled Peas

Imagine That!

- 1 pound of green peas, freshly shucked
- 6 ounces Chevre, Camembert or other soft, tangy and creamy cheese (set out to come up to room temperature)
- Dollop crème fraiche (sour cream)
- 4-6 sprigs fresh Lemon Thyme
- 1/3 cup water
- In a medium size pot, cook peas on medium heat until just past al dente (about 10 minutes)

» Remove peas, drain and place into a beautiful serving dish, immediately whipping in cheese. Top with swirl of crème fresh and garnish with Lemon Thyme and serve pronto! Easy Peezy Cheesey. And, we have achieved our ultimate human mission, world peace!

This requires a Celebration and a toast to humanity with Domaine Carneros' Tete du Cuvee, Le Reve!

A Votre Santé!

"Hope to see you on the Dance Floor in Wine Country!"

CPSIA information can be obtained
at www.ICGtesting.com
Printed in the USA
LVHW050011081020
668276LV00002B/18